"It has been my observation that vibrant growing Christians are those who are connected to a visible expression of the body of Christ—the church. This book deals with everything from the importance of the local church to the nature of commitment, choosing a good church, and much more. Added study questions make this a great resource for group study."

—**TEDD TRIPP**, pastor, conference speaker, author of *Shepherding a Child's Heart*

"Simply the best book to give new members, indeed new Christians in general, as they seek to understand how to live and to love the Lord and others in church. May this new edition reach far and wide to those who need wisdom and guidance for life in our heavenly Father's house."

—**LANCE QUINN**, Pastor-teacher, The Bible Church of Little Rock, Arkansas

"*Life in the Father's House* is well written, theologically sound, and rich with practical application. In today's evangelicalism, with so much based on pragmatism, 'felt needs,' or sociological trends, it is a joy and a refreshment to have such a resource as this to edify our people in the truth concerning the church. I highly recommend this book to pastors and lay leaders."

—**JEFF NOBLIT**, Pastor-teacher, First Baptist Church, Muscle Shoals, Alabama

"Whatever Dr. Mack writes is going to be helpful because he opens his theme and the living Word coincidentally. Then he applies timeless truths freshly to the testings and understandings of Christians in our twenty-first century. That is especially so in this book."

—**GEOFF THOMAS**, Pastor, Alfred Place Baptist Church, Aberystwyth, Wales

"For several years our church has given a copy of *Life in the Father's House* to everyone who has attended our membership class. It is simply the best book available on what it means to live out one's Christian faith as part of a community—as a member of the body of Christ. It is biblical, balanced, wise, easy to read, and surprisingly comprehensive for its length. An excellent primer for new Christians and a worthy reminder and challenge for seasoned saints."

—**WAYNE WILSON**, Pastor, Faith Bible Church, Acton, California; author of *Worldly Amusements: Restoring the Lordship of Christ to Our Entertainment Choices*

"*Life in the Father's House* was required reading for the membership class in our church when I was a senior pastor. It has a high view of Christ's bride, the church, during a time when entertainment and emerging churches have trivialized her. This book is an undeniably necessary read by all Christians."

—**JOHN D. STREET**, Chair, Graduate Program in Biblical Counseling, The Master's College and Seminary

"Choosing a book about church administration and worship can be as risky as picking wild mushrooms—the wrong kind poisons the consumer. *Life in the Father's House* administers the biblical antidote to such poisons. It stresses Scripture-guided and spiritually gifted leadership, membership, and service. With passion, accuracy, and clarity Wayne Mack and David Swavely provide leaders and laity alike with biblical teaching about the New Testament church at work and in worship. New members' classes should use the book as a trustworthy textbook, church leaders as a reference tool, and church members as a membership guide."

—**WILLIAM D. BARRICK**, Professor, The Master's Seminary, Director of Th.D. Studies

"The local church is under attack, not only by its opponents but also by 'friendly fire,' ready to abandon it for ineffectiveness in her Lord's call to make disciples. Wayne Mack and David Swavely do not fall into this trap of the devil that would reject the enduring wisdom and design of Christ. They address elements essential to making the local congregation the incubator of life, health, vitality, and functionality her Lord intends."

—**STANLEY D. GALE**, Pastor, Reformed Presbyterian Church, West Chester, Pennsylvania; author, *Warfare Witness: Contending with Spiritual Opposition in Everyday Evangelism*

"In a league of its own. For compact thoroughness and practical instruction in church membership, we need look no further. I highly recommend that every pastor, church leader, and church member read this outstanding book."

—**JERRY MARCELLINO**, Pastor, Audubon Drive Bible Church, Laurel, Mississippi; Moderator of F.I.R.E. (Fellowship of Independent Reformed Evangelicals)

"Pastors go to seminary to learn about the church, but where can church members go? They should go to this book. It is Church Membership 101, teaching not just facts, but a deep, practical love for the church of Jesus Christ."

—**JOEL JAMES**, Pastor-teacher, Grace Fellowship, Pretoria, South Africa

"Will help people participate in their church. In a day when congregations are full of lonely and uninvolved individuals who don't know how to engage the church body biblically, this book, newly revised, can start them on the right course."

—**DAVE DEUEL**, Academic Director, The Master's Academy International

"Members at Jubilee who are exposed to the biblical vision of the church in this book undoubtedly experience greater growth and maturity in love for their Savior. Once they see the love and commitment Christ has for his church (His body and bride), they soon realize that loving Christ *includes* loving the church and being deeply committed to it."

—**PAUL J. BANG**, Education Pastor, Jubilee Presbyterian Church (Korean-American Church), Conshohocken, Pennsylvania

"*Life in the Father's House* is medicine for the many ecclesiastical ills common today. Are you suffering from a spiritual malaise or a feverish distemper that threatens your church? Read this book and see what difference it will make. Pastors, give a copy to all your church members!"

—**CONRAD MBEWE**, Pastor, Kabwata Baptist Church, Lusaka, Zambia

"When I arrived at our church, this was the first book I asked every elder and deacon to read. Now we ask every prospective member to read this book. It is taking our whole church to a new level of commitment! I know of no other tool that gives such a great summary of what God expects of us in the local church."

—**TIM CANTRELL**, Senior Pastor, Honeyridge Baptist Church, Johannesburg, South Africa

LIFE IN THE
FATHER'S
HOUSE

LIFE IN THE
FATHER'S
HOUSE

REVISED AND EXPANDED

A Member's Guide to the Local Church

WAYNE A. MACK
DAVE SWAVELY

PUBLISHING
P.O. BOX 817 • PHILLIPSBURG • NEW JERSEY 08865-0817

Library of Congress Control Number: 2006934627

ISBN-13: 978-1-59638-034-9

This book is dedicated to my son,
Joshua Mack, who has been my friend
for many years and my copastor at
Fellowship Church of the Lehigh Valley
from 2000 to 2005.
—Wayne A. Mack

This book is also dedicated to
Faith Church in Sonoma, California,
who were my spiritual family and
my dearest friends for six wonderful years,
and to the new Faith Church in Malvern, Pennsylvania,
with whom I hope to serve the Lord for many years to come.
—David Swavely

CONTENTS

FOREWORD

In these days when many professing Christians think only of their personal relationship with Jesus Christ and, consequently, wander loosely without regard for their relationship to the church, it is critical to address the matter of corporate Christianity.

God has designed that we be joined not only to Him, but to His church, as well. The New Testament metaphors that depict the church are richly instructive in carrying the weight of this emphasis. God has called and placed all the redeemed into His church, which He has defined as

- a holy and royal priesthood offering spiritual sacrifices to God
- a chosen race belonging to God
- a separate nation whose King is the eternal God
- a temple indwelt by the Spirit of God
- a set of branches connected to Jesus Christ as the Vine
- a flock led by the Good Shepherd
- a household or family sharing the common life of the eternal Father
- a body of which the Lord Jesus is Head.

All these metaphors feature the common characteristics of unity and shared life and fellowship.

Believers compose one priesthood, one nation, one race, one temple, one plant, one flock, one family, and one body.

9

We have all been made one spiritually, and we belong together in communion, living out that oneness in local churches.

We are commanded not to forsake "our own assembling together," so that we can "stimulate one another to love and good deeds" (Heb. 10:24–25).

There has been a formidable supply of teaching on what believers should be in their own lives with the Lord, and there is plenty of data on the call and the duties of church leadership. What has been missing is the necessary instruction to believers about how they are to conduct themselves in the church to which they eternally belong and locally express their faith.

This helpful book lays out the crucial pattern for conduct in the fellowship that leads to the fulfillment of our Lord's desire in the church Christ "purchased with His own blood" (Acts 20:28).

John MacArthur
Grace Community Church
Sun Valley, California

INTRODUCTION

church (church) **n. 1.** a building for public worship **2.** public worship; a religious service **3.** a particular sect or denomination of Christians **4.** church government, or its power, as opposed to civil government **5.** the profession of the clergy **6.** a group of worshipers.

Those definitions of the word *church*, taken from the Student Edition of *Webster's New World Dictionary* (1981) betray the confusion that exists in our day regarding that institution. We reflect the first five definitions when we say things like, "It's about time to redecorate the church," "I enjoyed church today," "My church is the Lutheran church," and "I believe in the separation of church and state." But not one of those meanings of the term *church* can be found in the Bible. Rather, the Greek word translated in that way (*ekklesia*) is used over a hundred times in the New Testament, and it always refers to "a group of worshipers," which is the *last* definition mentioned in Webster's!

The "church" in Scripture is not a building, a denomination, or an activity—it is a group of people. This is true of both the universal church, which is the group of people throughout the world who believe in Jesus Christ (Matt. 16:18; Eph. 5:25–27), and also the local church, which is the group of people who meet together in a particular location for worship (Matt. 18:17; 1 Cor. 1:2). The word *ekklesia* is used in both ways in the New Testament, but the latter meaning is

11

much more prevalent. So throughout this book we will be referring to "the church" in that sense—the local body of believers who meet together to worship God and serve one another.

Technically speaking, those people do not worship "at a church" or participate "in church"—they *are* the church! And if you are a member of the body of Christ, you do not "go to church" or "sit in church"—you are a part of the church who comes together for worship with the rest of the body. This is important to understand because the quality of a church is therefore not measured by the condition of its buildings or the appeal of its services, but by the state of the people themselves. They are the church, so the church is only as good as they are.

That is why this book is "A *Member's* Guide to the Local Church." Most of the people in a particular congregation are not church leaders; they are simply church members, or "laymen" as they have often been called. But almost all of the books written about the local church have been geared to leaders. One would have to search far and wide to find another book like this that speaks directly and extensively to the responsibilities of the "common" people who are part of a local church.

Because this book is written to meet that specific need, it therefore does not contain any discussion of certain issues that church leaders must decide upon, such as the mode of baptism or the form of church government. The truth contained here applies to the members of any body that seeks to obey the Scriptures, regardless of denominational affiliation or other distinctives.

Not only is the meaning of the word "church" misunderstood today, but many Christians are ignorant or confused regarding their roles and responsibilities in a local body. For example: Do you know why most churches have a membership process, and is there any substantial difference between a "member" and a "regular attender"? What kind of church should a Christian attend, and what are good reasons to leave one for another? What kind of relationship should you have with the leaders of your church, and what role should they play in your life? How can you keep the Sunday services from becoming routine? And how can you either cause or prevent a "church split"?

Those questions and many more are answered thoroughly in the following pages. We hope that by the time you are finished reading this book, you will completely understand what God wants you to do as a part of the local church and how He wants you to do it. Our prayer is also that you will put into practice each truth you learn, so that your *Life in the Father's House* will be pleasing to Him.

I

REALIZING THE IMPORTANCE OF THE LOCAL CHURCH

"JESUS—YES! CHURCH—NO!" So read a placard carried by a student. In this spiritually hungry age, the interest in the person of Jesus is unmistakable. . . . At the same time the popular image of the church is that of empty and decaying buildings, aged and female congregations, and depressed and irrelevant clergy. Thus the growing enthusiasm for Jesus seems tragically offset by the almost total disenchantment with the church.[1]

Those words written in the late 1970s by English pastor David Watson accurately captured the spirit of the times in evangelicalism. The "Jesus Movement" of the sixties and seventies had spawned hundreds of parachurch organizations devoted to proclaiming the Gospel and teaching the Bible, and in most cases those organizations redirected the focus of believers away from the local church. A generation of leaders was exercising their spiritual gifts in other contexts besides the assemblies they attended on Sunday. This parachurch "theft" and a society accelerating into secularism at breakneck speed combined to reduce the attendance in local churches to an all-time low.

The eighties and nineties, on the other hand, brought both good news and bad news for the institution called the local church. The good news is that interest in church was greater than it had been for many years (particularly in America), and many churches reported tremendous growth in the number of people who attended their services. The bad news is that this "church growth movement" had largely accommodated the use of secular marketing techniques and an unfortunate tendency to dilute or camouflage the more confrontational features of the biblical message.[2] Therefore it had also fallen far short of producing commitment to the church in the lives of many, as illustrated in an intriguing book by William Hendricks called *Exit Interviews*.

Hendricks chronicles the failure of the "church growth movement" to keep people in the church, as the back cover of the book explains.

> There's a dark side to recent reports of surging church attendance in North America. While countless "unchurched" people may be flocking in the front door of the church, a steady stream of the "churched" is flowing quietly out the back. It's estimated that 53,000 people leave churches every week and never come back![3]

The book documents those claims through current statistics and numerous interviews with individuals who have left the church. The trend that it describes is sad indeed, but what is even more alarming about the book is the author's own opinions about the importance of the local church, which are woven throughout his interpretations of the interviews. Even though he makes several statements to the effect that he does not want to minimize the importance of the church, it is clear that he considers it to be only one of many *options* for the spiritual growth of believers.

> Despite glowing reports of surging church attendance, more and more Christians in North America are feeling *disillusioned* with the church and other formal, institutional expressions of Christianity.
>
> That's not to say that these "back-door believers" have given up on the faith. On the contrary, they may be quite articulate regarding spiritual matters. Indeed, some have remarkably vibrant spiritual lives and touchingly close friendships with a kindred spirit or two. But in the main, they tend to nurture their relationship with God apart from the traditional means of church and parachurch.
>
> "Impossible!" some will reply. "One simply cannot grow as a Christian unless one is part of a church, a local body of believers." So conventional wisdom would have it. . . .[4]

> Why dredge up something that puts a negative face on Christianity [i.e., the interviews]? As believers, shouldn't we dwell on the positive, on the edifying things that God is doing among and through His people? Yes, but the questions assume that nothing edifying is taking place, when in many cases that's exactly what is happening: God is doing His marvelous work in someone's life, even apart from the church—believe it or not.[5]

Referring to those he talked to who have left the church completely, the author says,

> After languishing for a while where they were, they chose to get out and find a better way. . . .[6]

17

Quite often they described themselves as moving closer to God *but further away from the church!*[7]

Finally, he devotes a chapter to addressing the "dropouts" he has interviewed and any readers who have also left the church. Here is his thoughtful message to them:

I am extremely reluctant to shake my finger in your face and say, "You turn right around and get yourself back in a church!" I don't know your circumstances. It may be that there are lots of alternatives around you, in which case I certainly would encourage you to explore them diligently until you find something that works. . . .[8]

Tradition holds that you cannot grow apart from a church. How, then, will you proceed (assuming that you want to proceed)? A few of the people I have interviewed have moved forward by standing tradition on its head and taking spiritual sustenance wherever they can find it—from books, magazines, television and radio ministries, a sympathetic friend or two, perhaps the arts and music, maybe volunteer work. Over time, they've become quite resourceful at finding ways to meet God apart from a local church . . . .[9]

I don't blame you for walking out.[10]

Exit Interviews was written by a respected, well-known Christian author and published by a conservative Christian publisher. It also hovered for quite some time in the top ten lists for Christian book sales. It is safe to say from those facts that the general regard for the local church among professing Christians at the close of the twentieth century had not improved much since the dreary sixties and seventies.

This trend has continued into the new century, unfortunately, and has even reached new lows. In 2005 George Barna, one of the most well known Christian leaders in America, published a book called *Revolution*, which is subtitled *FindingVibrant Faith Beyond the Walls of the Sanctuary*. In this book Barna commends the growing numbers of Christians who are "serving God" with no connection to a local church and even suggests that many others should follow their lead. He begins the book with an admiring portrait of a "committed Christian" who plays golf every Sunday morning instead of attending church and fills the rest of the book with quotes like this:

> "Scripture teaches us that devoting your life to loving God with all your heart, mind, strength, and soul is what honors Him. Being part of a local church may facilitate that. Or it might not."[11]

> "I am not called to attend or join a church."[12]

This contemporary indifference toward the church represents a gargantuan shift from long-standing values held by those throughout history who have called themselves the people of God. If *Exit Interviews* or *Revolution* had been written in any other century than our own, they would have likely been met with a chorus of righteously indignant protests from the Christian leaders of the day. They may have even been labeled "heresy" by our forefathers, who called people who left the church *apostates* rather than "back-door believers" or "revolutionary Christians."

Consider, for example, some statements from the three most recognized names in the history of our faith. Augustine said, "He cannot have God for his father who does not have the church for his mother." Martin Luther wrote, "Apart from the church, salvation is impossible."[13] And John Calvin's *Institutes of the Christian Religion*, which is the most widely read and treasured work since the apostolic age, contains these impassioned assertions about the local church:

> Because it is now our intention to discuss the visible church, let us learn even from the simple title "mother" how useful, indeed necessary, it is that we should know her. For there is no other way to enter into life unless this mother conceive us in her womb, give us birth, nourish us at her breast, and lastly, unless she keep us under her care and guidance until, putting off mortal flesh, we become like the angels (Matt. 22:30). Our weakness does not allow us to be dismissed from her school until we have been pupils all our lives. Furthermore, away from her bosom one cannot hope for any forgiveness of sins or any salvation. . . . God's fatherly favor and the especial witness of spiritual life are limited to his flock, so that it is always disastrous to leave the church.[14]

> The Lord esteems the communion of his church so highly that he counts as a traitor and apostate from Christianity anyone who arrogantly leaves any Christian society, provided it cherishes the true ministry of Word and sacraments.[15]

Augustine, Luther, and Calvin merely represent the thousands of Christian leaders throughout the centuries who believed the church is absolutely indispensable to our growth as Christians. Apparently our day has brought a tremendous change in the way people view the local church, especially when best-selling books imply repeatedly that we can grow just as well without it. But what does the Word of God say about the church of God? Our authority is neither prevailing thought nor the dogma of fallible theologians.

Rather we must find out what God thinks about this institution He has designed from the Book He has written to us.

Is it possible to have a vibrant spiritual life and successfully nurture our relationship with God apart from a local church? Is it just "conventional wisdom" that tells us we must be a part of one? Is it possible to move closer to God and farther away from the church? Are there "lots of alternatives" to the church when it comes to our spiritual growth? And are those who forsake all church involvement truly blameless for that choice?

The answer to all those questions, according to Scripture, is a resounding *no!* Far from being only one of many options for the Christian, *the church is the primary means through which God accomplishes His plan in the world.* It is His ordained instrument for calling the lost to Himself and the context in which He sanctifies those who are born into His family. Therefore God expects (and even demands) a commitment to the church from everyone who claims to know Him.

Even a cursory reading of the New Testament makes clear the centrality of the church in the biblical record. Jesus Christ proclaimed that He would build His church (Matt. 16:18), invested in it the authority to act with the imprimatur of heaven (Matt. 18:17–20), and ultimately revealed that His plan was to fill the world with local bodies of believers (Matt. 28:18–20). Most of the epistles are written to local churches, and three of the others written to individuals (1 and 2 Timothy and Titus) discuss how the local church should function. Finally, the wonders of Revelation were expressly intended for seven local churches in Asia Minor and sent to them by the apostle John at the command of the risen Christ (Rev. 1:4, 11).

No single verse proclaims the importance of the local church more powerfully than 1 Timothy 3:15, and that verse will serve well as a framework for a discussion of this doctrine in Scripture. There Paul says to Timothy, "I write so that you may know how one ought to conduct himself in the household of God, which is the church of the living God, the pillar and support of the truth." Paul wanted his young apprentice to understand the gravity and significance of his instructions, and so he referred to the local assembly of believers by four descriptive terms designed to emphasize its importance to God. These terms are still appropriate designations for the church, and an understanding of them should help us to share Paul's love and respect for this holy institution.

THE HOUSEHOLD OF GOD

The word "household" comes from the Greek *oikos*, which can mean either a dwelling place ("house") or an immediate family ("household"). Both meanings are applied to the church in Scripture, and both provide profound testimony to its divine origin and significance.

The Church Is God's Dwelling Place

If Paul used the word in the sense of a dwelling place, then it testifies to the fact that God Himself lives in and among His church. The church itself is the house of God. Please understand that we are not talking about the church *building*. The very words "house of God" conjure up images of an old deacon looking down upon us when we were children and saying, "No running in the sanctuary, young man—this is the house of God!" (Of course, we could run in the gym or in the halls, which were a part of the same building—but there was something especially holy about the room with the pulpit and pews.)

That old deacon was misusing the term "house of God," because it does not refer to a building at all, except in a metaphorical sense. The term is an allusion to the Old Testament tabernacle and temple, which are both often called by that name in Scripture (e.g., John 2:16; Acts 7:47). It therefore refers to the fact that, throughout history, God has chosen to work with groups of people and to manifest His presence in a special way when they assemble together.

In 1 Corinthians 3:16–17, Paul says to that whole church (not to individuals), "Do you not know that you are a temple of God, and that the Spirit of God dwells in you? If any man destroys the temple of God, God will destroy him, for the temple of God is holy, and that is what you are." He also says to the same group, "We are the temple of the living God; just as God said, 'I will dwell in them and walk among them; and I will be their God, and they shall be My people'" (2 Cor. 6:16). And Ephesians 2:19–22 says that we are "God's household, having been built upon the foundation of the apostles and prophets, Christ Jesus Himself being the corner stone, in whom the whole building, being fitted together is growing into a holy temple in the Lord; in whom you also are being built together into a dwelling of God in the Spirit."

The application of these verses to our discussion should be obvious: If we want to be where God is, we need to be in His church, for that is where He dwells. And the way we relate to Him is largely dependent upon the way we relate to His church, for it is the house He has built with His own hands (1 Peter 2:5).

The Church Is God's Family

The more likely meaning of the word "household" in 1 Timothy 3:15 is that of a family, because Paul used it that way in verses 4, 5, and 12 of the same chapter. The idea of being a part of God's family is not new to most Christians—we speak often of being "born again" into it, refer to God as our heavenly Father, and praise Him for adopting us as sons and making us His heirs (Rom. 8:15–17). We sing, "I'm so glad I'm a part of the family of God." Seldom (if ever) do we think of that "family of God" as the local church, but that is what the phrase means in this verse.

No doubt Paul used this phrase in order to convince Timothy of the importance of right conduct in the church. If elders and deacons are required to have their households in order (vv. 4, 5, and 12), how much more does God's own household need to be in order! But his language leaves us with an additional lesson pertinent to this discussion. Not only do we need to be in His church if we want to be where God is, but we also need to be in His family if we want to consider Him our Father. With Paul's words in mind, how could people call God their Father while refusing to be a part of His family? Yet that plain contradiction essentially describes the position of those who say they have faith and salvation apart from the church.

THE CHURCH OF THE LIVING GOD

The emphasis in this second description of the church falls on the words "of the living God." The church proceeded from *God* and belongs to *God*. This divine Originator and Owner of the church is *the* God—the only true God. And in contrast to the temples of dead pagan idols, Paul says that this church is of the *living* God. So at all times, He is personally and actively involved in its operation and enterprises.

Throughout the New Testament, God makes it clear to us that the church is His dearest creation and possession. In fact, each member of the Holy Trinity is repeatedly portrayed as treasuring it above all other earthly institutions.

God the Father has revealed His love for the church by His sovereign election of it before the foundation of the world

(Eph. 1:4–5; Rev. 13:8) and in the promises He gave to Abraham and the other patriarchs, many of which have been fulfilled at least partially in the New Testament church (Acts 2:39; Gal. 3:6–9). The Father paid the ultimate price for the church by sending His beloved Son to die (John 3:16; 1 John 4:14), so that it is said to have been "purchased with His own blood" (Acts 20:28). He participates continually in the fellowship of the church (1 John 1:3), and it functions primarily for the purpose of bringing Him glory (Eph. 3:21).

The Son of God "also loved the church and gave Himself up for her" (Eph. 5:25; cf. Titus 2:14). He laid down His very life for His sheep (John 10:11–16). Therefore God has made Him "the head of the church" (Eph. 5:23; cf. 1:22), and it is repeatedly called "the body of Christ" (Eph. 4:12; cf. 1 Cor. 12:12). Jesus has promised to be personally present when the church meets to enact His process of loving discipline (Matt. 18:20) and when it goes forth to carry out His command to make disciples of all nations (Matt. 28:19–20). The church is also where His beloved ordinance of Communion is observed regularly in commemoration of His death (Luke 22:17–20; 1 Cor. 11:23–26).

Finally, *the Holy Spirit* initiated the New Testament church at Pentecost through marvelous signs and wonders (Acts 2:1–4) and confirmed the inclusion of the Gentiles by a repeat performance (Acts 10:44–48). He brings each member into the body of Christ through His miracle of regeneration (1 Cor. 12:13; John 3:6–8) and guarantees their eventual glorification (Eph. 1:13–14). In fulfillment of the promises of Christ in John 14, the Spirit empowers the members of the church, indwells them, and illumines their minds to the truth of the Scriptures, which He Himself produced through the prophets and apostles (vv. 16–17, 26; cf. 2 Peter 1:21; Heb. 2:4). He also works to promote unity and peace in the body

(Eph. 4:3) and provides the various spiritual gifts that enable it to function properly (1 Cor. 12:7–11).

First Peter 1:1–2 mentions all three members of the Trinity when it says that the churches throughout Asia Minor were "chosen according to the foreknowledge of God the Father, by the sanctifying work of the Spirit, that you may obey Jesus Christ and be sprinkled with His blood." The entire Godhead is deeply and intimately involved in the origin and operation of the church. Therefore, we who would be "called sons of the living God" (Rom. 9:26) must be involved in His church. And no doubt the stern warnings of the book of Hebrews apply today to those who would spurn such involvement: "Take care, brethren, lest there should be in any one of you an evil, unbelieving heart, in falling away from the living God" (Heb. 3:12) and, "It is a terrifying thing to fall into the hands of the living God" (Heb. 10:31). We would do well to remember that this jealous living God is the One to whom the church belongs.

THE PILLAR OF THE TRUTH

Paul's next descriptive name for the church—"pillar" (from the Greek *stulos*)—tells us that it actually *holds up* the truth. Or to put it in more graphic (and perhaps shocking) terms, God's truth is not able to stand without the church. If the pillar of a building is removed, as Samson proved in his last act in the Philistine temple (Judg. 16:29–30), the building will topple and the people inside will be injured or killed. The implication of Paul's words is that the truth would fall into disaster if the church did not exist.

Of course that fearful event will never occur, because God has promised that His church will always endure (Matt. 16:18). He has ordained that both the truth and its "pillar" will stand forever (cf. 1 Peter 1:25; Eph. 3:21). But as Paul's words were designed to help Timothy grasp the gravity of right conduct in the church, so they are meant to convince us of the indispensable role that the church plays in our individual lives. Our own relationship to God and His truth *is* in mortal danger if church does not occupy its intended place in our lives. So when we consider those who abandon the church as a means of spiritual growth, it is highly unlikely that they are truly holding to the truth or cultivating a meaningful relationship with God by themselves. In light of 1 Timothy 3:15, it is much more likely that their faith has crumbled—because they have torn away the pillar that holds up the truth.

How does the church function as a pillar of the truth? The following are some ways that the church has been designed to uphold the truth of God:

Revelation. God chose to reveal the truth of the New Testament in and through the church. Paul wrote,

> To me, the very least of all saints, this grace was given, to preach to the Gentiles the unfathomable riches of Christ, and to bring to light what is the administration of the mystery which for ages has been hidden in God, who created all things; in order that the manifold wisdom of God might now be made known through the church to the rulers and the authorities in the heavenly places. This was in accordance with the eternal purpose which He carried out in Christ Jesus our Lord. (Eph. 3:8–11)

First Corinthians 12:28 says, "God has appointed in the church, first apostles, second prophets," and those are the men whose mouths and pens brought us His inspired Word (cf. Eph. 4:11). We should add, however, that the apostles and prophets served only as *the foundation* for the church (Eph. 2:20), and therefore that ministry of revelation is not ongoing today. The faith was "once for all delivered to the saints" in the first century (Jude 3; cf. Rev. 22:18–19), and therefore any church claiming to add subsequent revelation to the Scriptures is a false church.[16]

Proclamation. Although the church has finished its task of revealing the truth of God, it remains the instrument He has chosen to proclaim that truth to the world. As R. B. Kuiper wrote,

> Rome is in grievous error when it asserts that the church dispenses *saving grace itself.* But so are they in error who overlook the fact that the church must dispense *the means of saving grace.*
>
> God employs but one means to impart faith to men. It is His Word, the Bible. "Faith cometh by hearing, and hearing by the Word of God" (Romans 10:17). It is the sacred duty of the church to proclaim that Word. When it pleases the Holy Spirit to call sinners effectually by the Word as preached by the church, believers come into being. It is because of this important role of the church in the birth of believers that the church deserves to be denominated *the mother of believers.* Believers are born of God through the church.[17]

Obviously most gospel proclamation takes place outside the gathering of the church, but in Scripture it is always the church that initiates and sanctions such evangelism. Acts 13:1–3 tells us that the church at Antioch officially ordained Paul and Barnabas as missionaries, and Paul said later that Titus "has also been appointed by the churches to travel with us" (2 Cor. 8:19).

God has also designed the church to be the institution in which the Word is proclaimed to believers. Acts 2:42 says that the early church gathered regularly to study the apostles' teaching, and Ephesians 4:11–12 tells us that the church has been given "pastors and teachers, for the equipping of the saints for the work of service, to the building up of the body of Christ."

Administration. The church also acts as a pillar of the truth because only in it can God's people enjoy the structure and order He has devised for their worship and growth. God has never provided instructions for how a parachurch organization should function, let alone for how people can worship and grow totally on their own. But He has revealed an exhaustive plan regarding how the church should function for His glory and the good of its members (1 Tim. 3:15). That plan includes guidelines for baptism and the Lord's Supper (which are ordinances of *the church*), giving, leadership, worship, preaching, men's and women's roles, and myriad other essential issues (most of which we will discuss in the remainder of this book). The bottom line is that God has designed the church to be the context in which we move from sinfulness to holiness. Attempting to grow in Christ outside of the church is like trying to learn to swim without ever getting into the pool!

Protection. Finally, the church upholds the truth by protecting it from error. It judges the teaching of false prophets, declares them to be divisive, and renounces them if they persist in their heresy (Rom. 16:17; Titus 3:9–11; 2 John 9–11). When a dispute arises between two brothers, the church is called to adjudicate their case and determine who is right and wrong (1 Cor. 6:1–6). And the church also protects the truth from the harmful influence of those who live ungodly lifestyles.

Jesus said that if such a person refuses to respond to repeated confrontation, we should "tell it to the church; and if he refuses to listen even to the church, let him be to you as a Gentile and a tax-gatherer. Truly I say to you, whatever you shall bind on earth shall be bound in heaven; and whatever you loose on earth shall be loosed in heaven" (Matt. 18:17–18; cf. 1 Cor. 5; 2 Thess. 3:6–15). Only the church is given the ability and authority by God to take that kind of action against error and sin, and without it the truth is left unprotected to a great degree. When the pillar is gone the truth is much more likely to be misrepresented, compromised, and ignored.

THE SUPPORT OF THE TRUTH

At first glance this description of the church seems identical to the last, but it does translate an entirely different Greek word (*hedraioma*) and communicates a significantly different shade of meaning. In light of its etymology and its coupling with "pillar," this Greek word probably means "foundation," as most lexical tools indicate. Some scholars have been reluctant to translate it that way because the Roman Catholic Church has used that translation as support for the idea that the truth *proceeds from* the church. In fact the translation "foundation" lends no validity to that Catholic doctrine, because the word contains no idea of *source* whatsoever. Rather it speaks of *stability* and *permanence*.

One theological dictionary says this about another form of the word used often in classical Greek:

> The adj. *hedraios* (derived from *hedra*, seat, chair, abode, place) . . . originally was used by men in the sense of sitting,

sedentary, and then more generally for firm, unshakeable, stable. Thus *hedraios* is used . . . in questions about absolute certainty and the ultimate basis of all existence (especially by Plotinus). The reference is always to something secure and permanent in itself.[18]

Why did Paul choose this word in his attempt to help Timothy realize the primacy and importance of the local church? He wanted Timothy to know that the church is the one institution God has promised to preserve throughout all time. It will always endure, and even succeed, regardless of the many assaults and catastrophes that threaten it. Jesus affirmed this fact in the most definite terms when He said, "I will build My church; and the gates of Hades shall not overpower it" (Matt. 16:18). And Ephesians 3:21 says that God will receive "glory in the church and in Christ Jesus to all generations forever and ever."

The truth that the church will always be built and blessed by God Himself provides a tremendous source of hope and confidence to us as Christians. It also presents a convincing argument for the idea that we should direct our energies and efforts primarily toward the edification and growth of the local church rather than organizations and institutions outside of it. God has promised to preserve and bless the church, but endeavors of Christians in those other arenas will not necessarily bear lasting fruit.

For example, many Christians (and Christian leaders) today are expending tremendous amounts of energy to stem the rising tide of secularism and moral relativism in America. Our culture has indeed become sadly post-Christian, and may become increasingly anti-Christian in the future. But the Bible never commands us to commit our greatest efforts to ensuring that the society we live in remains tolerant to

Christianity. And if we invest our efforts and hope in that pursuit, we will only open ourselves to tremendous disappointment, because we have no guarantee that our government will ever be tolerant toward Christians. God may very well allow it to become like Nazi Germany or Communist Russia. If He does, that would not be "the end of the world" for us believers, nor would it be a horrible blow to God's purposes. God's glorious plan of building His spiritual kingdom will go on undaunted, regardless of whether America retains its religious liberty.

If, however, we are fighting primarily for the salvation of souls and the edification of God's people (particularly in the context of the local church), our hope will never be shaken, because those blessed works will continue even if the culture around us takes a nose dive. Because the church acts as a permanent foundation for the truth of God, it will always remain an exciting and fulfilling place in which to serve Him.

> *The dwelling place and family of God.*
> *The body greatly beloved by each member of the Trinity.*
> *The indispensable pillar holding up the truth of the Scriptures.*
> *The incomparably stable, timeless foundation of our service for Christ.*

What more could be said about the importance of the church than what Paul communicated in these four vivid descriptions? Perhaps now you can understand why Christian leaders through the ages like Augustine, Luther, and Calvin have said, with the Westminster Confession, that "outside the church there is no ordinary possibility of salvation" (XXV, 2). We are justified by faith alone in Christ alone, and not on the basis of our works (Gal. 2:16; Eph. 2:8–9), and those men believed and taught that truth consistently and passionately.

But they also recognized that "faith without works is dead" (James 2:14–26) and that God not only justifies His elect but also sanctifies them by creating in their hearts a love for Him, for His Word, and for His people. Consider these verses:

> By this all men will know that you are My disciples, if you have love for one another. (John 13:35)

> The one who says he is in the light and yet hates his brother is in the darkness until now. The one who loves his brother abides in the light and there is no cause for stumbling in him. But the one who hates his brother is in the darkness and walks in the darkness, and does not know where he is going because the darkness has blinded his eyes. (1 John 2:9–11)

> They went out from us, but they were not really of us; for if they had been of us, they would have remained with us; but they went out, in order that it might be shown that they all are not of us. (1 John 2:19)

That last verse is speaking primarily about false teachers, but in principle it applies to all those who claim to be Christians and separate themselves from the church. Such people may possibly be disobedient believers, but it is more likely that they are not really believers. As we said earlier in this chapter, how could someone claim God as Father and have no interest in being a part of His family? On the contrary, one of the primary evidences of being born again is a desire to worship God with His people in the church. This "work" of ours proves that the work of God is taking place in our hearts and lives. Jesus said "I will build My church," and He does so by saving people and placing them as "living stones" in "God's building" (1 Peter 2:5; 1 Cor. 3:9). Acts 20:28 refers to "the church of God, which He purchased with His own blood," and Ephesians 5:25 says that He "loved the church and gave Himself up for her." The purpose of Christ's saving love and sacrifice was to bring people into His church!

So it only remains to ask ourselves whether the church is as important to us as it is to the Lord, and how we can make sure that it holds the rightful place in our lives and ministries. The remainder of this book will help us to understand what God expects of us in relation to His church, but for now these words from Robert Saucy will serve as a fitting summary and conclusion to what we have discussed so far:

> Throughout the course of history God has worked in a variety of ways through individuals, nations, and peoples. The focus of His present work is the church. That which was begun in the Scriptures, as men and women were called to acknowledge the Lordship of Christ, continues today in fulfillment of Christ's promise to build His church. Not only is Christ building His church, but it is the primary instrument through which He ministers in the world. As Christ was sent by the Father, so the church bears the ambassadorial role for its Lord as sent ones with a message of reconciliation to the world (Jn 20:21).
>
> The reality of the church as the instrument of God and as His primary concern today is met with skepticism and incredulity, not entirely without reason. Amid the blustering crosscurrents of our time, which have shaken all of man's institutions down to the foundations—and in some cases are periling even these, if they have not already been destroyed—the church has not stood unscathed. That which bears the name of God has suffered confusion with the rest. The resultant widespread weakness and uncertainty have caused many to turn aside, rejecting with castigation the church as the locus of God's activity. While it

is true that certain forms of church life, accretions of time more than biblical patterns, may be rejected, the follower of Jesus Christ cannot profess allegiance to Him *and* deny His church. What is needed far more than denunciations is constructive criticism and renewed effort to seek God's ways in which one may be a part of the building process. For His purpose still remains: His church will endure.[19]

QUESTIONS FOR DISCUSSION AND APPLICATION

1. When the church is called "the body of Christ" in Scripture, what does that imply about the importance of the church? How about "the family of God"?

2. Acts 20:28 says that God purchased the church "with His own blood." How does that speak about the importance of the church? Also discuss Ephesians 5:25–27.

3. Why does the Westminster Confession say that "outside the church, there is no ordinary possibility of salvation"? What two extremes do you think this statement is trying to avoid?

4. How would you rate the importance of the church in your own personal life? How important is it compared to other human institutions, like family, government, school, parachurch organizations, sports teams, and clubs? How about compared to your hobbies and other leisure activities?

2

COMMITTING OURSELVES TO
CHURCH MEMBERSHIP

Several years ago, Dr. Jay Adams was fielding questions at a counseling conference in San Diego. One man raised his hand and asked, "Should we practice church discipline on people who are not members of our church?"

"No, of course not," answered Jay in his inimitable style of loving firmness. "Church discipline is only for believers." A questioning rumble passed through the room, and so he explained further, "People who are not members of a church should be treated like unbelievers, because they are treating themselves as unbelievers."

A stronger wave of murmurs swept through the audience, and a multitude of hands shot up.

"What if your church doesn't have church membership?" was the next question. The person who asked it went on to explain that he was from a certain denomination (as were *many* of the other attenders at the conference) the leaders of which did not believe in having a church roll of any kind because they felt that was an unnecessary, legalistic requirement to place upon their people. So, in effect, Jay Adams had just

7

told several hundred pastors, counselors, and committed laypeople that they should all be treated as unbelievers!

Jay had known about that denomination's policy before he made his comments, and his intention was not to insult those brothers and sisters. Rather he wanted to get their attention and cause them to think about the issue of church membership. It apparently worked, because they listened intently as he went on to explain and qualify his provocative comments. Several pastors from that same denomination approached him afterward and said that they had been convinced by his reasoning and were planning to implement membership in their churches.

Though we may not use the same words that Jay did on that day (at least not without a lot of qualification!), we agree with him that church membership is a very important issue. In fact, we believe that it is best for every local church to have a membership system, and that every Christian should commit himself or herself to membership, when the opportunity is available. This chapter will discuss three basic reasons why church membership is biblical and wise: (1) the command for commitment to a local church, (2) the obligation of obedience to the leaders of a local church, and (3) the privileges of partnership with a local church.

THE COMMAND FOR COMMITMENT

The Bible clearly commands every believer to be deeply involved in the lives of other believers. Hebrews 10:24–25 says, "Let us consider how to stimulate one another to love and good deeds, not forsaking our own assembling together, as is the habit of some, but encouraging one another; and all the more, as you see the day drawing near." God says that we are not to forsake "the assembling," but He does not mean only that we must attend church services regularly. The meaning of the passage is much fuller than that, as revealed by the other commands it contains. If we are not considering (or planning) how to stimulate others to love and good deeds, involved heartily in that process, and encouraging others more and more all the time, then we are disobeying the Lord.

The primary context in which God wants this involvement to take place is the *local body of believers,* and so the commitment called for is also a commitment to the church. Almost all the "one anothers" of the New Testament are given directly to local churches and are intended to help those churches be what God wants them to be. It is not enough for us to say that we are merely a part of the universal or invisible church (all those who believe throughout the world, regardless of church affiliation). We must also commit ourselves to a local or visible group of God's people. In fact, just as every believer in Old Testament times was required to identify himself outwardly with God's covenant people (Gen. 17:9–14, 23–27; 34:14–17), so the New Testament does not contain even a hint of someone who was truly saved but not a part of a local church. As R. B. Kuiper wrote,

> It is clear that in the days of the apostles it was universal practice to receive believers into the visible church.
>
> What could be more logical? He who believes in Christ is united with Christ. Faith binds him to Christ. He is a member of Christ's body, the invisible church. But the visible church is but the outward manifestation of that body. Every member of the invisible church should as a matter of course be a member of the visible church. Extremely significant in this connection is Acts 2:47—"And the Lord added to the church daily such as should be saved." Not only does the Lord Christ require of those who are saved

that they unite with the church; He Himself joins them to the church. And the reference is unmistakably to the *visible* church.

Does it follow that he who is outside the visible church is necessarily outside Christ? Certainly not. It is possible that a true believer because of some unusual circumstance may fail to unite with the church. Conceivably one may, for instance, believe in Christ and die before receiving baptism. But such instances are exceptional. The Scriptural rule is that, while membership in the church is not a prerequisite of salvation, it is a necessary consequence of salvation. Outside the visible church "there is no ordinary possibility of salvation" (Westminster Confession of Faith, Chapter XXV, Section II).[1]

Commitment to a local church is not only the assumed responsibility of everyone claiming to be part of the universal church, but it is also the only appropriate response to the truths we learned in chapter 1 about the importance of the church. Some of the verses mentioned in that discussion were referring to the invisible, worldwide body; but those constitute only a small minority of the uses of the Greek word *ekklesia* in the New Testament. Out of the 110 times that word is translated "church," only 17 are clear references to the universal church, while 90 undoubtedly denote the local church. Even in those few times when the New Testament writers are referring to the universal church, the idea of the local church cannot be eliminated from the word because the two are so inextricably linked, the one being the visible manifestation of the other.

If the church is the household of God, the pillar and support of the truth, the body for whom Christ died, and the current form of His kingdom and His people, then every person who claims to belong to Him should belong to the local church. Charles Spurgeon spoke pointedly about that truth over a hundred years ago.

> I know there are some who say, "Well, I have given myself to the Lord, but I do not intend to give myself to any church." Now, why not? "Because I can be a Christian without it."
>
> Are you quite clear about that? You can be as good a Christian by disobedience to your Lord's commands as by being obedient? There is a brick. What is it made for? To help build a house. It is of no use for that brick to tell you that it is just as good a brick while it is kicking about on the ground as it would be in the house. It is a good-for-nothing brick. So you rolling-stone Christians, I do not believe that you are answering your purpose. You are living contrary to the life which Christ would have you live, and you are much to blame for the injury you do.[2]

Many people who attend churches today—perhaps *most* of them—are unfamiliar with a biblical commitment to the church. If they would merely become aware of its importance and make that commitment, then the problem of church membership would be solved in their lives because they would be willing to join the church to which they are committing themselves. Or if they are in a church that does not have church membership, they would do whatever they can in that situation to be committed to the body. But we realize that there are also many Christians who are *already committed* to a local church and would say that there is no need for them to go through some kind of interview process and be placed on a roll. They say that commitment to the church does not necessarily have to be reflected in a formal membership process. Among them are some leaders of churches themselves, such as those in the denomination mentioned at the beginning of this chapter.

The remainder of this chapter is directed as much to those people as it is to the uncommitted. We believe that biblical principles and sound wisdom support the idea of specifically, publicly, and even legally identifying those who are a part of the church. Ideally every church should have such a membership list that contains the names of every believer who worships there regularly. And every believer who worships there should be willing and eager to be identified with the church in that way.

THE OBLIGATION OF OBEDIENCE

At both of our churches, the elders have asked every believer who has chosen to worship with us to join the church through a formal membership process. That process involves a class explaining membership, an interview with one of the church leaders, and a public commitment and welcome during one of our services. Most other churches have a similar process developed and encouraged by their leaders. This alone should be sufficient reason for any Christian in those bodies to become a church member, based on the clear teaching of these passages:

> But we request of you, brethren, that you appreciate those who diligently labor among you, and have charge over you in the Lord and give you instruction, and that you esteem them very highly in love because of their work. Live in peace with one another. (1 Thess. 5:12–13)

> Obey your leaders, and submit to them; for they keep watch over your souls, as those who will give an account.

Let them do this with joy and not with grief, for this would be unprofitable for you. (Heb. 13:17)

So if the leaders of your church want you to become a member, then God Himself wants you to become a member, because God uses them to lead you into His will. And notice that last passage does not only tell you to obey and submit to your leaders, but it contains a third command that is often overlooked. It says that we should help our leaders watch over our souls *with joy*. We are not only to do what they tell us to do (unless they tell us to sin), but we are also to do whatever we can to make their oversight easier for them to accomplish.[3] Church membership unquestionably makes it easier for the leaders of the church to shepherd the flock, for the following reasons. These reasons should not only help church attenders see the importance of becoming members, but also convince some leaders themselves to establish and encourage a membership process:

Membership is essential to an orderly administration of the church. God has invested in the church His manifold grace, the truth of His Word, and the souls of His redeemed people. The church must be a faithful steward of those treasures, and to do so it must put careful thought into developing and maintaining its structure and organization. Why should businesses striving for short-lived financial gain be administered more circumspectly than an institution laboring to lay up treasures in heaven (John 6:27; Matt. 6:19–21)? On the contrary, we should "let all things be done properly and in an orderly manner" (1 Cor. 14:40), and membership plays a vital part in any church structure. Eric Lane wrote,

> The church is likened in the Bible sometimes to a body, sometimes to a family or household, sometimes to a kingdom,

sometimes to an army. For any of these organisms to function properly order of some kind is required. The same applies to the church. The church is not just a loose collection of individuals, it is a closely-knit structure like a human body (Eph. 4:16) and has therefore to be rightly organized. For such ordering it needs to know exactly who belongs to it. A family which sat down to its meal-table or locked its doors at night, not knowing who was supposed to be there and who not, would be an extremely strange phenomenon. An army battalion which did not know whom to expect on parade would soon be in chaos. If the church is to be a true family and an effective fighting force it needs to know who exactly belongs to it.[4]

Membership clarifies the difference between the church and the world. Or, as Jay Adams implied, it helps us to know who should be treated as "believers" and who should be treated as "unbelievers." Membership will never tell us who *is* and *is not* a true Christian, because there will always be nonmembers who are saved and members who are unsaved (cf. Matt. 7:21–23; 13:36–43). In other words, the membership roll of the invisible church will always be different than the membership roll of the visible church, to some degree. But at times it becomes necessary to have some criteria by which to decide whether or not someone should be *treated* as a Christian (or a "brother" or "sister," as the New Testament puts it). One example would be marriage—a believer should not marry an unbeliever (2 Cor. 6:14); another example is divorce—different instructions are given to those married to unbelievers (1 Cor. 7:15; 2 Cor. 5:17); and a third example is elder qualifications—they must have "children who believe" (Titus 1:6).

In situations like that, how can church leaders and others determine whether someone is in the category of a believer or an unbeliever? Biblical theology and practical wisdom indicate that a mere profession of faith is not sufficient in this regard. But a commitment of accountability to the church, along with a credible profession of faith, is a safer way to go. Patient instruction is required, however, because so many Christians today have not been taught about church membership, and many have been in churches that do not even practice it. So for instance, if a young couple wants a pastor to perform their wedding, he can ask them early on if they are members of a good church. If the young lady is, but the young man is not, then the pastor can inquire about the reasons and instruct him about the importance of membership. If after such instruction the young man refuses to commit himself to the church, however, then the pastor would have to consider him in the category of an unbeliever and refuse to marry them, because otherwise he would be creating an "unequal yoke."

The question of who is to be treated as a believer may be most pertinent to the issue of church discipline (see chapter 8). If a "brother" or "sister" is living a sinful lifestyle and refuses to respond to private confrontation, then the church is commanded by God to deal with the sin (Matt. 18:15–17; 1 Cor. 5). But how do we know whether a particular attender is a "brother" or "sister" without a system by which the person can officially join or reject the church? And how can we officially put the offending party *out* of the church if he or she has never officially entered into it? If people who are to be treated as unbelievers commit sin, our response to that would not be to excommunicate them, but to evangelize them!

Legal considerations also come into play in regard to church discipline. In recent years, several churches have been sued by people who have been named from the pulpit, and questions have been raised about the legality of disciplining nonmembers.[5] In light of those recent developments, it is probably not prudent to exercise the discipline process on those who are not members. So if the church leaders allow a large percentage of their flock to be nonmembers, their hands may be tied to a great degree when any of those people fall into sin. They may be unable to obey several important commands in Scripture and powerless to remove from the body the ruinous influence of an immoral or divisive person.

Membership causes the visible church to better reflect the invisible church. This point is similar to the previous one but has more of a theological nature. R. B. Kuiper expressed it clearly and eloquently.

> The visible church is glorious insofar as it resembles the invisible church. Visibility and invisibility are two aspects of the one church of Jesus Christ. For that simple and conclusive reason the visible church must manifest the invisible. Admittedly, the resemblance of the one to the other is never perfect. But in some instances the visible church is no more than a caricature of the invisible. Then it is inglorious. In a great many instances the visible church seeks feebly to reflect the invisible. Then its glory is dim. By the grace of God there are also instances in which the visible church concertedly emulates the invisible. Such a church is truly glorious.[6]

For the sake of its testimony before the world, the local church should look as much as it can like Christ's spiritual body, which enjoys perfect unity (John 17:22–23), wholehearted submission to Him (Eph. 5:22), and absolute stability (Matt. 16:18). That means no one should be allowed to join the church who denies the gospel, but it also means that everyone who is a part of God's spiritual family should be a member of the local church. If that were the case, those who merely attend the church from time to time with insincere hearts would not be considered a part of the church as they often are today. They also would be less likely to stain the church's reputation by calling it "my church" to the world while living ungodly lives.

Two final reasons support the fact that it is wise for church leaders to emphasize membership.

Membership promotes involvement from those on the "fringes" of the church. This is especially true when they realize they must make a choice between being committed or uncommitted. An emphasis on membership provides a way for people to take a big step in their sanctification by moving from "the crowd" into the "congregation." They are also more likely to serve in the church when they have made the investment of a membership commitment. As Jesus said, "Where your treasure is, there will your heart be also" (Matt. 6:21, Luke 12:34).

Membership provides an opportunity to educate people about the nature and distinctives of the church. This will keep regularly involved people from being ignorant of matters such as church discipline and spiritual gifts, even when they are not frequently discussed from the pulpit. At our churches, we have found that people can attend for a long time before being confronted with particular doctrines of importance, merely because those truths have not come up in the exposition for quite a while. So we view the membership process as a vital ingredient in our attempts to be "admonishing every man and teaching every man with all wisdom, that we may present every man complete in Christ" (Col. 1:28).

THE PRIVILEGES OF PARTNERSHIP

Charles Spurgeon once told his congregation this story about church membership:

> I well remember how I joined the church after my conversion. I forced myself into it by telling the minister, who was lax and slow, after I had called four or five times and could not see him, that I had done my duty. And if he did not see me, I would call a church meeting myself and tell them I believed in Christ, and ask them if they would have me.[7]

Why was the young Spurgeon "banging on the door" of the church to get in? No doubt he knew that commitment to a local church and obedience to leaders were necessary to his spiritual growth, and he greatly feared the God who had issued those commands. But there also may have been another compelling reason for him to force his way into membership in the church—the *benefits* he would gain by being a part of it.

Church membership is not only a commitment on the member's part to the church, but it is a commitment on the church's part to the member. Both the church as a body and its leaders vow to care for the member by providing the following advantages:[8]

Ministry opportunities. Leadership, teaching, evangelism, handling of funds, music, ushering, and even such seemingly mundane tasks as nursery care and grounds keeping should be performed by those who love Christ and are committed to the church. That is because the members of the body are gifted by the Spirit for the purpose of accomplishing the work of the ministry (1 Cor. 12; Eph. 4:11–16). One way to make sure that takes place is by making membership a requirement for such service. Many churches do just that, so in many cases those who refuse to become members are basically saying that they are not willing to fulfill the ministries for which they may be gifted by God. On the other hand, those who are members have the freedom to obey God in any way He calls them to serve.

Helpful services. One church we know has a biblical counseling ministry staffed by over twenty men and women trained to apply the Scriptures to the cares of the soul. So many people have expressed a desire to be served in this way that the church has had to limit availability of the counseling to members alone. Likewise, the overworked pastoral staff often has to make choices about whom they can offer their time, and those who are members take priority over those who are not. The church has even been forced to limit weddings on the premises to members because of the great demand and a limited staff.

Every church may not be as swamped with needs as that one is, but it is likely that many find themselves in a similar situation. And other churches may even choose (as we have in some cases) to intentionally limit their services to members in order to encourage that commitment. Either way, in many local bodies those who have officially committed themselves find it easier to be ministered to by the church.

Loving accountability. Another benefit of belonging to a local church is that its leaders and members can hold us accountable according to the process of church discipline mentioned earlier in the chapter. The possibility of being confronted for our sin or put out of the church is not something we naturally view as beneficial, but that is only because our viewpoints are clouded by our sinful flesh. Actually we should welcome and even seek such accountability, because it is a powerful tool that God uses to mold us into the image of His Son.

Confrontation is an act of love that greatly benefits the one confronted, and even the harshest discipline is enacted for the good of the offender. Consider these verses:

> Let the righteous smite me in kindness and reprove me; it is oil upon the head. (Ps. 141:5)

> Do not reprove a scoffer, lest he hate you. Reprove a wise man, and he will love you. Give instruction to a wise man, and he will be still wiser. Teach a righteous man, and he will increase his learning. (Prov. 9:8–9)

> Whoever loves discipline loves knowledge, but he who hates reproof is stupid. (Prov. 12:1)

> He who neglects discipline despises himself, but he who listens to reproof acquires understanding. (Prov. 15:32)

> Better is open rebuke than love that is concealed. Faithful are the wounds of a friend, but deceitful are the kisses of an enemy. (Prov. 27:5–6)

> I have decided to deliver such a one to Satan for the destruction of his flesh, that his spirit may be saved in the day of the Lord Jesus. (1 Cor. 5:5)

> Among these are Hymenaeus and Alexander, whom I have delivered over to Satan, so that they may be taught not to blaspheme. (1 Tim. 1:20)

> My son, do not regard lightly the discipline of the Lord, nor faint when you are reproved by Him; for those whom

the Lord loves He disciplines, and He scourges every
son whom He receives. (Heb. 12:5–6)

Accountability and confrontation from other individual
believers can take place in our lives if we are not members of
a church, but as we discussed earlier, the later stages of the
process often cannot. So if we should persist in some sin (God
forbid), all of the means that God has designed to pull us away
from it are not available to us. So in effect, an unwillingness
to join a local church is tantamount to saying we are not in-
terested in divine accountability in our lives.

Considering the privileges of partnership in the local
church, every person who is not a member of one should be
"banging on the door" to get in. Combined with the command for commitment to the church and our obligation to
obey our leaders, you can see why membership is not an option for a true believer. That's why it is true in a sense that
those who refuse church membership "treat themselves as unbelievers" (especially after being taught the truths above), because they are willingly disobedient to the commands of God
and have foolishly denied themselves the benefits of God's
community.

Eric Lane says that the believer's relationship to the
church is analogous to a marriage. He likens Christians who
refuse church membership to a man and woman who merely
declare themselves married and move in together without ever
submitting to a legal marriage ceremony.

They have only thought of themselves and not of the society of which they are a part. Marriage is a public affair, because, however private a matter individuals may think it to
be, other members of the community have a right to know
who belongs to whom and who is whose wife or husband.

A society in which everyone behaved as this couple would be sheer chaos. Moreover, their selfishness in fact rebounds on their own head, because, by refusing registration, they preclude themselves from certain benefits the state grants to married folk.[9]

To borrow the same analogy of marriage, we need to honor Christ by being His bride in every sense—outwardly as well as inwardly, visibly as well as invisibly, and officially in the local church as well as spiritually in the universal body.

QUESTIONS FOR DISCUSSION AND APPLICATION

1. Do you think that churches should have a membership roll, and a process by which people can join the church? Why or why not?

2. If your church has a membership roll, are you on it? Why or why not?

3. What membership vows or commitments did you make when you became a member, or would make if you became a member? How do you think making those vows might affect your life?

4. What are some ways that you have lived out those vows in the body, and what are some ways you plan to do so in the future?

3

CHOOSING A GOOD CHURCH

When Christians realize the importance of the church and look for one in which to be involved, they often run into a confusing plethora of choices. The number of denominations claiming to be a part of the Christian religion throughout the world was estimated at 20,800 in 1980,[1] and that number has most certainly grown substantially since then. In many American communities, there are more churches than schools, grocery stores, or even restaurants. (In some of the "Bible belt" towns, there seem to be more churches than all three of those combined!)

So, realizing the importance of the church and membership in it is not the end of the war for many believers—they must then fight the excruciating battle of finding a church in which they can worship and serve God. This chapter is designed to help such people know what to look for in a local church. For those of us who are already involved in good churches, it will also provide a standard by which we can judge the quality and progress of those bodies. We will get a good idea of what the local church is meant to be by looking back at the first Christians in Jerusalem. Acts 2:42–47 describes those believers in this way:

> And they were continually devoting themselves to the apostles' teaching and to fellowship, to the breaking of bread and to prayer. And everyone kept feeling a sense of awe; and many wonders and signs were taking place through the apostles. And all those who had believed were together, and had all things in common; and they began selling their property and possessions, and were sharing them with all, as anyone might have need. And day by day continuing with one mind in the temple, and breaking bread from house to house, they were taking their meals together with gladness and sincerity of heart, praising God, and having favor with all the people. And the Lord was adding to their number day by day those who were being saved.

The early church described in that passage was successful in every area. It was vibrant, pleasing to God, and growing by leaps and bounds. Therefore, we can learn a lot from it. Also, because it embodied the principles taught throughout the New Testament that apply to all churches in all times, we know that our church bodies today can become like it in emphases and philosophy.

In case there might be misunderstanding, we are *not* saying that we should or even can do everything exactly as the church did in Jerusalem. There were differences even between the various churches in New Testament times, and we believe there is room for differences among churches today. We cannot be expected to copy their example in every detail. If we did, we would have to throw away our suits, sweaters, and dresses and buy robes; we would have to stop speaking English and learn Greek or Aramaic; we would have to sell our cars and walk everywhere, with sandals on our feet instead of Nikes or wing tips.

So God doesn't want us to do everything as the early church did,[2] but there are certainly some basic features that characterized the church in Acts 2 that should characterize the church in the twentieth century as well. They could be summarized by saying that a good local church exhibits *a devotion to the apostles' teaching, a God-centered focus,* and *a loving concern for the needs of people.* The presence of those characteristics made the early church exciting and effective, and they must be present in any church today for it to be truly successful in the eyes of God.

A DEVOTION TO THE APOSTLES' TEACHING

The first characteristic of the early church mentioned in Acts 2:42, and the most foundational trait for any God-honoring church to have, is a continual devotion to the apostles' teaching. The New Testament church was founded as a direct result of the teaching of the apostles (Acts 2:14–41), and after that our text says that the believers in Jerusalem "were continually devoting themselves" to it. The Greek verb translated "continually devoting" (*proskarterountes*) literally means "to be strong towards." That tells us that the early believers were earnestly and perpetually dedicated to the apostles' teaching; it also may speak of enthusiasm and excitement toward it.

The Greek word translated "teaching" (*didache*) encompasses both the *content* and the *manner* of the apostles' teaching. Understanding both of those fully will help us to evaluate biblically any church today.

The Content of the Apostles' Teaching

What exactly did the apostles teach? We find the answer to that question in the rest of the book of Acts, and in the rest of the New Testament, because all of that was written by the apostles or those who worked with them. It is also found in the entire Old Testament, because that was the inspired Scripture the apostles studied and taught from. Acts 17:2 says that Paul went according to his custom to the synagogue of the Jews and for three Sabbaths reasoned with them from the Scripture. The Scripture that he had at that time was the Old Testament.

So the apostolic teaching is everything contained in the Word of God—or "the whole counsel of God," as Paul put it in Acts 20:27 (NKJV). It includes the truth about God's character—the sovereignty of God, the justice of God, the love of God, the power of God, the grace of God, and the omniscience of God. It includes the truth about election, predestination, justification, redemption, irresistible grace, the perseverance of the saints, sin, righteousness, salvation, judgment, forgiveness, the virgin birth of Jesus Christ, the sinless life of Jesus Christ, the substitutionary atonement, His glorious resurrection, and His ascension to the right hand of God the Father.

The apostolic teaching also includes practical admonitions and instructions about marriage, finances, employer-employee relationships, parent-child relationships, missions, and responding to authorities. In short, the apostolic teaching includes "everything pertaining to life and godliness" (2 Peter 1:3). So when we approach any topic that falls into the category of "life and godliness," the primary issue is not what the great theologians of the church say, it is not what tradition says, it is not what the educated people of our day say, and it is not what the well-known preachers in the church say. Rather, the issue is *what does the Word of God say?* That is what the early church cared about, and that must be the emphasis in our churches today. John MacArthur has written,

56

The church's primary function is to proclaim God's Word. I've heard people criticize Grace Church saying, "There's too much preaching and teaching at Grace Church, and not enough of other things." I don't see how there could ever be too much preaching and teaching! That could happen if everyone knew all of God's revelation, but that is impossible. The reason we put so much emphasis on preaching and teaching is that they help everything else to happen. We have to know what the Bible says about something before we know how to act. We won't know how to worship, pray, evangelize, discipline, shepherd, train, or serve unless we know what the Word of God says.[3]

A good test of the soundness of a particular church is whether it could be open to that kind of criticism (that there is "too much teaching"). If that is the case, the church probably realizes the importance of communicating truth and has committed itself to that biblical emphasis. Another good question to ask in evaluating a church would be whether or not the teaching there includes all the truths listed above. If so, that body is probably making a concerted effort to give apostolic teaching its rightful place.

The Manner of the Apostles' Teaching

How did the apostles teach? We get a glimpse of the manner of their teaching in Peter's sermon recorded in Acts 2:14–36, and we should desire to be part of a church that practices the same kind of teaching. Peter's message was effective and pleasing to God because of the following characteristics:

It was relevant. In verses 14–15, Peter began his sermon by relating to the events occurring in and around his audience. He answered the questions they were asking and provided the specific information they needed to understand their current situation.

It was biblical and expository. In verses 16–21, 25–28, and 34–35, Peter quoted passages from the Old Testament. He then proceeded to explain the meaning of all those passages and make application from them to the lives of his hearers.

It was Christ-centered. The subject of Peter's message was the person and work of Jesus Christ (vv. 22ff.), and that same subject dominated all subsequent preaching by the apostles (cf. 1 Cor. 2:2; 15:1ff.; 2 Cor. 4:5; Col. 1:28).

It was specific and personal in application. Peter addressed his listeners directly, saying "*you* yourselves know" (v. 22), "*you* nailed [Christ] to a cross" (v. 23), and "let all the house of Israel know for certain that God has made Him both Lord and Christ—this Jesus whom *you* crucified" (v. 36). He did not merely lecture them about facts, but vigorously sought to impress the truth upon their souls.

It was authoritative. Peter did not merely share his opinion for the consideration of his audience. He boldly declared the nonnegotiable facts of the gospel. He commanded them to "listen" to the truth about the man who was "attested" (or proved) to them by "miracles and wonders and signs" (v. 22).

It was purposeful in intent. His words were designed to persuade those who heard him; he wanted to produce an effect in them through the power of the Holy Spirit, and to incite them to act upon the truth they heard (vv. 37ff.).

That was the kind of teaching the apostles presented to the early church, and it was that kind of teaching the church devoted itself to continually. Those people did not gather together to be entertained; they did not gather to talk about their feelings in a kind of "group therapy" session; they did not gather to discuss their opinions or otherwise pool their ignorance; and they did not gather to contemplate the ideas of Socrates, Epicurus, Plato, or any other secular authority. Rather they gathered together with the primary intent of learning from the apostles' teaching.

Furthermore, the early Christians tested everything by the standard of the apostles' teaching. Any belief or practice that was not in accord with it was rejected immediately, and any religious organization that did not abide by it was considered a false church.[4] John wrote the following on behalf of himself and the other apostles:

> Beloved, do not believe every spirit, but test the spirits to see whether they are from God; because many false prophets have gone out into the world. . . . They are from the world; therefore they speak as from the world, and the world listens to them. We are from God; he who knows God listens to us; he who is not from God does not listen to us. By this we know the spirit of truth and the spirit of error. (1 John 4:1–6)

Ephesians 2:20 says that the church has been "built upon the foundation of the apostles and prophets, Christ Jesus Himself being the corner stone." There are no more apostles and prophets today—the foundation of their teaching has been laid and does not need to be laid again. But we must be sure that the building of the church conforms to the foundation that was laid for it by the apostles. If any building is to stand, it must take the shape of its foundation—and if any church today is to stand the test of God's Word, it must adhere completely to the apostles' teaching.

In 1 Timothy 6:20, Paul told his young protégé Timothy, who was then pastoring the church at Ephesus, "Guard what has been entrusted to you, avoiding . . . the opposing arguments of what is falsely called 'knowledge.'" And in his second letter to Timothy, Paul wrote,

> I solemnly charge you in the presence of God and of Christ Jesus, who is to judge the living and the dead, and by His appearing and His kingdom: preach the word; be ready in season and out of season; reprove, rebuke, exhort, with great patience and instruction. For the time will come when they will not endure sound doctrine; but wanting to have their ears tickled, they will accumulate for themselves teachers in accordance to their own desires; and will turn away their ears from the truth, and will turn aside to myths. (2 Tim. 4:1–4)

In that passage Paul speaks of people who heap to themselves teachers who will tell them what they want to hear. They don't want to hear the apostles' teaching, but they want to hear the newest idea, philosophy, or fad from the world that will make them feel better about themselves and their lifestyles. But such was not the case in the Jerusalem church described in Acts 2, and it must not be the case in our churches today. A good church is one where the people desire and respond to biblical teaching and preaching, and where the leaders are committed to providing that for them regularly and perpetually.

Unfortunately, our churches today often give the Bible *titular authority* rather than *functional authority*. Many of them relegate the Word of God to a role not unlike that of the Queen of England. She has the title of a ruler but participates very little in the actual governing decisions of the country. The real power and influence reside in the Prime Minister and in Parliament. Similarly, many churches today prominently display the Bible and claim to believe it, but when it comes to the everyday functions of the church, the Bible is not their final authority. So, as we are considering commitment to a particular church, we need to find out whether it is characterized by doing the Word or by merely hearing it (James 1:22–25). As John Calvin wrote concerning Acts 2:42,

> Do we seek the true Church of Christ? The picture of it is here painted to the life. He begins with doctrine, which is the soul of the Church. He does not name doctrine of any kind but that of the apostles which the Son of God had delivered by their hands. Therefore, wherever the pure voice of the Gospel sounds forth, where men continue in the profession thereof, where they apply themselves to the regular hearing of it that they may profit thereby, there beyond all doubt is the Church.[5]

A GOD-CENTERED FOCUS

Acts 2:43 says that in the church at Jerusalem "everyone kept feeling a sense of awe." The power of the apostles' teaching and the numerous signs and wonders done among the people deeply affected their attitude toward God. One commentator notes, "The conviction of sin that followed Peter's preaching was no momentary panic, but filled the people with a lasting sense of awe. God was at work in them; they were witnessing the dawn of a new age."[6] The awe of the people was directed toward God, of course, and this awe could be more accurately called "a respectful fear." The Greek word translated "awe" is *phobos*, which is almost always translated "fear" in the New Testament (cf. Acts 5:5, 11).

This "fear" of God that the people experienced, however, is not an irrational state that produces the uncontrolled behavior reflected in our modern use of the word *phobia*. Rather it was a solemn recognition of the presence of a holy and loving God in their lives, which motivated them to obey Him gladly (vv. 44–46) and to praise Him continually (v. 47). Thus the "awe" they experienced was a mixture of gratefulness, respect, and dread as they saw God for who He was and recognized His presence with them. In a word, they were constantly *worshipping* God.

We are not experiencing the dawning of a new age today, or the supernatural signs that accompanied it; but we can and should experience the same kind of awe and worship toward God that the early church had. Psalm 2:11 says, "Worship the Lord with reverence, and rejoice with trembling." Our attitude toward God should include joy and gratefulness, but those good feelings must always be tinged with the respect and fear that is due to the Ruler of the universe. Without that respect and fear, we can become flippant toward God and fail to give Him the honor He deserves (cf. 1 Sam. 2:30).

That important truth is communicated very clearly in 1 Peter 1:17. Prior to that verse, Peter was discussing the loving election of God and the great salvation He has lavished upon His people (vv. 1–12); then he began emphasizing the response of obedience and holiness that befits the children of God (vv. 13–16). Verse 17 begins with the Greek conjunction *kai*, which can often be translated "even," if the context allows. In this case it does, so Peter's words can read this way: "Even if you address as Father the One who impartially judges according to each man's work, conduct yourselves in fear."

Here the word *phobos* means the same thing it does in Acts 2:43—a reverential awe of God. And so Peter is saying that even though we are grateful and happy to have God as our loving Father (a term of warmth and intimacy), we still must realize that He is also the holy Judge, and we must be careful to obey Him with a grave reverence. Or, as one commentator says, when Christians "call God Father, they should remember his character and not allow familiarity to be an excuse for evil."[7]

That principle must be true of a church as well. The attitude governing its ministries and communicated to its people must be one of awe toward God. That means He must be taken very seriously, and it also means that He must be preeminent in everything that happens in the church. Only then can a local body be truly God-centered like the one at Jerusalem. The leaders and members of a church must realize that it does not exist primarily for the benefit of man, but for the glory of God and His Son Jesus Christ. Consider these verses carefully:

> Everyone who is called by My name, and whom I have created for My glory, whom I have formed, even whom I have made. (Isa. 43:7)

> For [by] Him [Christ] all things were created, both in the heavens and on earth, visible and invisible, whether thrones or dominions or rulers or authorities—all things have been created [by] Him and for Him. (Col. 1:16)

> Worthy art Thou, our Lord and our God, to receive glory and honor and power; for Thou didst create all things, and because of Thy will they existed, and were created. (Rev. 4:11)

All things exist primarily for the glory of God, rather than for our benefit. And that includes the church, which was created predominately for His honor and not for our happiness (Eph. 3:21). Unfortunately, however, that is not the focus of most churches today. Their primary purpose is to solve people's problems or meet people's needs, rather than bringing glory to God. The following contrasts can help us to determine whether a church is God-centered or man-centered in its focus.

A man-centered church will follow extrabiblical traditions that make people more comfortable because of their familiarity, but a God-centered church will jettison unbiblical traditions and be wary of any that might somehow obscure the simplicity of Christ (cf. Mark 7:6–13; 1 Cor. 4:6; 2 Cor. 11:3).

A man-centered church will hesitate to address certain doctrines or avoid them entirely because they might be offensive to some members, but a God-centered church will boldly and faithfully proclaim "the whole counsel of God" (Acts 20:27 NKJV; cf. 2 Tim. 3:16–17; 4:1–2; Titus 2:15).

A man-centered church will choose worship and teaching styles primarily on the basis of people's preferences, but a God-centered church will endeavor to conform its services as closely as possible to the biblical model, regardless of what people may think or how many people might come (cf. Rom. 1:16; 1 Cor. 4:1–3; 2 Cor. 10:3–4; 2 Tim. 4:3–5).

A man-centered church will encourage people to receive counsel from ungodly "experts" (either directly or through the integration of their ideas with Scripture), but a God-centered church will point them to the sufficient answers provided by our jealous Lord in His Word (cf. Ps. 1:1; Col. 2:8; 2 Peter 1:3).[8]

A man-centered church will not practice church discipline in regard to sinning members because that process is too "harsh" or "unloving," because it might diminish attendance or giving, or simply because it involves too much hard work. A God-centered church, however, will reveal true love for its members and obedience to Christ by carrying out discipline when it is necessary (cf. Matt. 18:15–17; 1 Cor. 5; 2 Thess. 3:6–15).[9]

Finally, a man-centered church will have very little emphasis on prayer and will seldom be engaged in corporate prayer (again because it is such hard work), but a God-centered church will be like the early believers in that they will be "continually devoting themselves . . . to prayer" (Acts 2:42; cf. Eph. 6:18; 1 Tim. 2:1, 8; James 5:16–18).

A LOVING CONCERN FOR THE NEEDS OF PEOPLE

Although it is committed to the teaching of sound doctrine above all other pursuits, and although it exists more for the glory of God than for our good, a good church also cares deeply about the needs of people. For this concern to be genuinely biblical, it must be kept in balance with the priorities of sound teaching and worship, so that the needs of people never become more important than God Himself or His truth. On the other hand, a church that is committed to teaching and worship but shows no concern for the true needs of people is imbalanced and unbiblical. As Paul said in 1 Corinthians 13:2, "If I have the gift of prophecy, and know all mysteries and all knowledge; and if I have all faith, so as to remove mountains, but *do not have love*, I am nothing." And Proverbs 29:7 says, "The righteous is concerned for the rights of the poor, the wicked does not understand such concern."

The church described in Acts 2 was both balanced and biblical in this regard. They exhibited great love and care for each other and for those outside their number who did not yet know the Lord.

A Concern for Others in the Body of Christ

Acts 2:42 says that the members of the church at Jerusalem "were continually devoting themselves . . . to fellowship"; verse 44 says they "were together"; and verse 46 says they were regularly "taking their meals together." They had developed close relationships, and they spent a significant amount of time with one another. This "togetherness" was not only physical, of course, but also emotional and spiritual—verse 46 says they were "continuing with one mind." They were bonded to each other in answer to their Lord's prayer "that they may all be one" (John 17:21).

This loving unity was not only expressed by spending time together in spiritual fellowship, but also through sacrificial giving to meet the physical needs among them. They "had all things in common; and they began selling their property and possessions, and were sharing them with all, as anyone might have need" (vv. 44–45). This was not an early form of communism but a voluntary, generous sharing of resources that took place every time a specific need arose.[10] What probably made the needs significant at that time was that Jews from every nation had been visiting Jerusalem for the feast of Pentecost (Acts 2:5), and many of them who became Christians remained in Jerusalem to learn from the apostles and to fellowship with the church. Some of them were certainly without jobs from that point on, away from their homes or disenfranchised from their families (or both).

The believers who were better off sold the property and possessions that they didn't need and freely gave the money to those who were less fortunate. In twenty-first century America, most of what we have are things we don't need—yet many of us find it tremendously difficult to give up anything for others! The sacrifices made by the early Christians was an indication that God was working among them and that they were a true church.

Any true church today will exhibit the same kind of concern for the needs of its members. The love of Christ and the power of the Holy Spirit will compel God's people to give generously for this purpose, so that no true church will ever be able to blindly ignore the legitimate financial or physical needs of its people. Nor would a good church ever relegate their "deacons' fund" to a minuscule fraction of the budget as a token gesture to the poor. The fact is, a good way to test the caliber of a certain church is to find out how much money it has allocated for caring for the needy (if any) and how that amount compares to the overall budget.

We are so grateful that our churches have significant funds set aside for mercy ministries, and that no member with a legitimate need is ever turned away without help. But we know of many young, growing churches that have not set aside *any* money for that purpose because they are focused on a building project, the growth of their pastoral staffs, or other pursuits that have taken precedence at this time.

That should not be happening. God clearly commands the church to care for the needs of its members. This command is explicit and implicit throughout the many references in both testaments to God's concern for the poor and needy.[11] It is also implied in the family motif that Scripture continually employs in regard to the Christian community. The church is referred to as the household (or family) of God in 1 Timothy 3:15; the Scriptures refer repeatedly to God as our Father; and the most common term used in reference to Christians in the New Testament is *adelphos*, which means "brother" (or "brethren" in its plural form). It is used well over three hundred times in reference to fellow believers, and the significance of that fact for our discussion is that we must care for our spiritual brothers and sisters in the same way we care for our physical family. Certainly most of us would empty our bank accounts before we would allow our mothers or our siblings to starve or to go without necessary medical treatment, and we should have the same attitude toward our brothers and sisters in Christ.

First Timothy 5:8 says, "If anyone does not provide for his own, and especially for those of his household, he has denied the faith, and is worse than an unbeliever." That verse is referring specifically to a person's physical family. In the context, however, the application of its truth spills over into our spiritual family as well because the church is commanded to meet the needs of widows who cannot care for themselves sufficiently. So a good church is one that cares for its widows and any other members who are in need.

A Concern for Those Outside the Body of Christ

Acts 2:47 says that the early church was "having favor with all the people. And the Lord was adding to their number day by day those who were being saved." In the book of Acts, the Greek term for "people" (*laos*) most often refers to the unsaved inhabitants of a particular area (cf. 4:1–10). So, in this verse, it is probably a general reference to the unbelieving Jewish population in Jerusalem. Of course, "those who were being saved" were formerly unbelievers who came to Christ through the Gospel message. From this we know that the church in Jerusalem was having a tremendous impact on the world around them, and no doubt that impact flowed from a great love for their unsaved neighbors.

In our churches today we cannot necessarily expect to have the approval of the unbelievers in our communities (the favor enjoyed by the church at Jerusalem didn't last very long itself), and we also cannot expect God to be adding converts to our fellowships every single day. But we can be like the early Christians by lovingly and faithfully proclaiming the Gospel to the world around us. A good church will always be doing that.

As John MacArthur says, "For many Christians, the nearest they come to penetrating their community is driving to church in a car that has a fish sticker on the back window!"[12] And, unfortunately, the nearest some churches come to evangelism is talking about it once in a while or holding a yearly "revival" service attended almost entirely by their own members. A truly biblical church, however, will repeatedly emphasize the necessity of evangelism and regularly equip its members to do it (cf. Matt. 28:19–20; 1 Thess. 1:8). So one way to evaluate a church is to inquire about how many professions of faith they have had in the last year, or how many people have become members who were not formerly churchgoers. In our experience, we have encountered numerous churches that are very solid in doctrine, but rarely lead people to Christ. Surely this is not pleasing to our Lord Jesus, who came to seek and save the lost, and told us to make disciples of all kinds of people (Matt. 28:18–20).

DON'T SAY YES TO A NO CHURCH!

In his book *Handbook of Church Discipline*, Jay Adams coined a term for churches that refuse to practice church discipline even after repeated instruction and exhortation. He said we "should declare them to be 'no church' since they will not draw a line between the world and the church by exercising discipline."[13] "No church" is a strong term, but it is an appropriate one, because no matter how often a group of people call themselves a church, it means nothing if they are not functioning as a church, according to God's instructions. The local Rotary Club could decide to call itself a church, but that would not make it one! Unfortunately, many of the options facing believers today as they seek a place to fellowship fall into that category of "no church." They definitely fall into that category if they are not characterized by the essential qualities we have discussed in this chapter. So we are biblically obligated to choose a church that demonstrates a devotion to the apostles' teaching, a God-centered focus, and a loving concern for the needs of people.

That kind of church reflects the character of the body described in Acts 2, which was so pleasing to God and so greatly used by Him. One commentator summarizes the passage we have discussed in this way:

> Verses 43–46 give an ideal portrait of the young Christian community, witnessing the Spirit's presence in the miracles of the apostles, sharing their possessions with the needy among them, sharing their witness in the temple, sharing themselves in the intimacy of their table fellowship. Their common life was marked by praise of God, joy in the faith, and sincerity of heart. And in it all they experienced the favor of the nonbelievers and continual blessings of God-given growth. It was an ideal, almost blissful time marked by the joy of their life together and the warmth of the Spirit's presence among them. It could almost be described as the young church's "age of innocence." The subsequent narrative of Acts will show that it did not always remain so. Sincerity sometimes gave way to dishonesty, joy was blotched

by rifts in the fellowship, and the favor of the people was overshadowed by persecutions from the Jewish officials. Luke's summaries present an ideal for the Christian community which it must always strive for, constantly return to, and discover anew if it is to have that unity of spirit and purpose essential for an effective witness.[14]

QUESTIONS FOR DISCUSSION AND APPLICATION

1. On what basis did you choose the church you are now attending? What was important to you when you made that choice, and what was not so important?

2. Why is the teaching of God's Word so important in a church? How does it relate to the other ministries in a church?

3. With a humble and constructive attitude, evaluate your church based on the list of "God-centered" vs. "man-centered" on pages 64–65. What is your church doing well, and how do you think it could become more God-centered?

4. In what ways are the people in your church reaching out to needy Christians? In what ways are they reaching out to people who are not Christians? And how can you be involved those kinds of ministries?

4

RELATING TO CHURCH LEADERSHIP

Throughout the Old Testament, God provided leaders for His people Israel, and the welfare of that nation was largely dependent on the effectiveness of its leaders (cf. Prov. 29:12). How the people responded to their leadership was also a significant factor in whether the nation would be blessed or judged by God. In 1 Chronicles 16:22, God told the pagan nations surrounding Israel, "Do not touch my anointed ones, and do my prophets no harm." Unfortunately, God's people themselves often turned against their leaders, thus bringing condemnation upon themselves. Nehemiah 9:26–27 says, "But they became disobedient and rebelled against Thee, and cast Thy law behind their backs and killed Thy prophets who had admonished them so that they might return to Thee, and they committed great blasphemies. Therefore Thou didst deliver them into the hand of their oppressors who oppressed them."

God has instituted positions of leadership within the New Testament church as well, and He is greatly concerned that they be recognized and maintained in the manner He has prescribed in Scripture. He also is greatly concerned that the members of any particular local church understand and live out the biblical principles pertaining to their relationship with their leaders. Unfortunately, unbiblical extremes characterize many churches in this regard.

One extreme is an outright denial or ignorance of the need for a functioning authority structure in the church, and another extreme is an enslaving authoritarianism that cripples the body. As one writer explains,

> In evangelical circles today we are witnessing the abuse of ecclesiastical authority in two directions. There is, on the one hand, an abdication of church authority by some. Confronted with the individualistic, anti-law spirit of our time, cowardly church officers refuse to exercise the biblical oversight entrusted to them by Christ. In many circles authoritative preaching and corrective church discipline are conspicuously absent. Equally dangerous, however, is the tendency by others to overreact against such laxity. Church leaders lose sight of the fine line between the virtue of biblical counsel and guidance and the vice of usurping control over the conscience. Wise pastors recognize that parishioners who emerge from the social, moral, and domestic chaos of modern society need order and structure in their lives. In view of the Christian's struggle with uncertainty and confusion of life in a post-Christian environment, watchful shepherds of God's flock see the need for firm direction and predictability. Yet in grappling with these challenges, godly overseers can blur in the minds of their followers the distinction between God's Word and man's word and unwittingly shift the standard of God's will from the Bible to human pronouncements. Counsel becomes control, control becomes coercion, and coercion becomes tyranny over the conscience. Christian freedom is eroded as lay people become more and more enamored with the

decrees of elders and the commandments of men. It all has the appearance of wisdom, but it represents a slippery path into slavery.[1]

Both of those extremes occur frequently and are an unfortunate possibility in any congregation. The church leaders are certainly responsible to see that neither happens, but so are the members of the body. In fact, for the authority structure of a church to function as God designed, *each member* must be aware of his or her responsibilities to the leadership and diligently attempt to fulfill them (cf. 1 Cor. 12:12–30).

A verse that speaks clearly and directly to the issue of our relationship to church leaders is Hebrews 13:17: "Obey your leaders, and submit to them; for they keep watch over your souls, as those who will give an account. Let them do this with joy and not with grief, for this would be unprofitable for you."

The writer of Hebrews, through the inspiration of the Holy Spirit, summarizes our responsibilities to leaders by saying that we need to recognize their authority and help them to enjoy their ministry. A thorough understanding of the commands in this verse and other amplifying references will provide us with a complete picture of the relationship God wants us to have with those He has placed over us.

RECOGNIZING THE AUTHORITY OF LEADERS

The first half of Hebrews 13:17 enjoins us to obedience and submission to our leaders, and then provides some incentive for us to exercise those virtues.

The Command to Obey

"Obey your leaders," we are told by the inspired writer. Obedience to God and His ordained authorities is a common theme in the New Testament, but the Greek word for "obey" (*peitho*) is not the most commonly used term for that idea. Because of that, and because it is used so closely to the word "submit," it has a significant nuance. In the tense and voice used here, the Greek word *peitho* literally means "to be continually persuaded." It is always used in reference to a verbal proclamation or argument, and so the idea is clearly that we are required to constantly allow the teaching and counsel of our leaders to be very persuasive in our hearts and lives.

The writer of Hebrews probably chose this word to intentionally echo a statement he made earlier in the chapter. Verse 7 says, "Remember those who led you, who spoke the word of God to you; and considering the outcome of their way of life, imitate their faith." There he was speaking of the believers' responsibility to cling to the teaching of their former leaders (who were probably now dead), as opposed to being "carried away by varied and strange teachings" (v. 9). Verse 17 commands the Hebrew Christians to receive the words of their present leaders with the same vigor and fidelity.

The word "obey" in the verse does not *only* denote a willing reception of teaching and counsel, however. It also carries an undeniable connotation of compliance to directions. The Greek verb is clearly used that way elsewhere. James 3:3 says that "we put the bits in the horses' mouths so that they may *obey* us" (*peitho*).

But more importantly, the Greek word translated "leaders" is *hegoumenois*, which is used twenty-four times in the New Testament (usually translated "governor") to refer to secular authorities, such as Pilate and Felix. So, in its three uses in the book of Hebrews (13:7, 17, and 24), the King James Version rightly translates it as "them that have the rule over you."

This command to obey our leaders contains an unmistakable emphasis on the authority of their words in our lives, but does that mean we are required to comply unquestioningly with anything they tell us to do? Not according to John's third epistle. The apostle, in effect, tells his friend Gaius to *disobey* Diotrephes, who was apparently a duly appointed or elected leader in the church. John says that "Diotrephes, who loves to be first among them, does not accept what we say. . . . neither does he himself receive the brethren, and he forbids those who desire to do so, and puts them out of the church. Beloved, do not imitate what is evil, but what is good. The one who does good is of God; the one who does evil has not seen God" (3 John 9–11).

According to that passage, God does not want us to obey church leaders if they tell us to do evil; we should obey them only when they tell us to do good. If we are directed toward what is evil, then we must answer as Peter and John did to the Jews: "We must obey God rather than men" (Acts 5:29). The following questions will help us to determine whether we should obey our leaders in specific circumstances:

Is our objection a matter of conscience or merely preference? If we are questioning whether to follow our leadership in a particular area, we must ask ourselves why this is so. If, after concentrated study, we are firmly convinced from Scripture that their directions are unbiblical, then we have good reason to follow our conscience rather than their words. Keep in mind, however, that the evaluation of the conscience is based on the *knowledge* that our mind possesses (the Greek word for conscience means "to know with"), so emotions or feelings are not the issue in such decisions. A particular choice may be the right one even if we do not "feel right" about it (and vice versa). Unfortunately, in our sinfulness, our emotions often point us away from obedience rather than toward it.[2]

We must also be careful not to confuse the convictions of our conscience with our preferences. In fact, it is precisely in the matter of preferences that leaders need to make decisions in order for any church to run smoothly. For instance, the times of the worship services and the choice of musical styles in those services are matters of preference on which it would be impossible for everyone in the congregation to agree. We certainly should offer humble input to our leaders about such issues, but leaving early every week or refusing to sing would be examples of ungodly disobedience that would only foster disunity in the body.

Is their leadership causing us to sin, or is it confronting our sin? Certainly we should object if our leaders lay such burdens upon us that we cannot fulfill clear commands of Scripture, or if they want us to do something that is expressly contrary to the Word of God. But many times it seems that our objections to the teaching or rules of the church arise simply because we are fallen, sinful creatures who tend to resist any authority in our lives. (The worship of autonomy and independence in our culture does not help us to fight that tendency, either.) Or it may be that God is working through our leaders to expose an area of needed growth in our lives, and our sinfulness is resisting change in that area.

An example of an unfounded objection to church leadership is the matter of membership that we discussed in chapter 2. There are simply no good scriptural reasons for refusing to join a good local church, and there are tremendous benefits in being a committed part of a body of believers. Yet even sincere Christians often bristle when confronted by their leaders about the need to dedicate themselves to the church in that way. When we find ourselves resisting our leadership for some reason other than a biblical conviction, we would do well to hear the words of the apostle Paul to the Galatians: "Who hindered you from obeying [*peitho*] the truth? This persuasion did not come from Him who calls you" (Gal. 5:7–8).

Finally, is the leadership issuing commands or merely offering counsel? Because of the textual emphasis on authority in this command to obey our leaders, we can understand that it is primarily regarding the requirements they place upon us. These would include (among other things) accountability to clearly scriptural duties, permission to be involved in particular ministries, and matters of protocol necessary for the orderly administration of the church. What Hebrews 13:17 does not demand is that we comply or even agree with the *suggestions* proffered by our leadership. As we will discuss more thoroughly later, it would be wrong for us to allow our leaders to do all our thinking for us. Often it would be helpful to ask them whether we are required to "be persuaded" by their words. Are they saying, "We think you should do this," or, "You need to do this"?

That is not to say that the counsel of our leaders is unimportant. On the contrary, God has gifted them with special abilities and experience, enabling them to provide crucial insight that we ourselves often lack. Proverbs 15:22 says that "without consultation, plans are frustrated, but with many counselors they succeed." And Proverbs 20:18 urges us to "prepare plans by consultation, and make war by wise guidance." Not only are we commanded by Scripture to obey the dogmatic directions of our leaders, we are also commanded to consider very carefully the advice they have to offer.

The Command to Submit

Hebrews 13:17 says not only that we should obey our leaders, but also that we should "submit to them." This is the

79

only biblical occurrence of this Greek word (*hupeikete*), but we know that the root word (*eiko*) means "to yield" or "to place under." We also know that in classical Greek the word is often used to denote submission to authority.[3] Therefore, the basic meaning of the word is not very different from the word "obey." Why, then, does the writer of Hebrews mention it at all? Is he merely repeating the same command with a new word, or is there a difference in the meaning of the two commands?

The answer lies in the fact that the Greek word translated "obey" is in the middle voice, which gives it the *passive* sense of "allow yourselves to be persuaded." The word translated "submit," however, is an *active* verb (in the present tense), indicating that we must diligently and continually devote ourselves to the process of "placing ourselves under" our leaders. No doubt the Lord realizes that our tendency is to take a passive approach to our leadership, responding to them only when they expect something of us or when an individual leader "crosses our path" in some way. But He wants us to take an active approach to submission in which we constantly seek to be more submitted, or better submitted, to our leaders.

How can we obey this command? What does biblical submission to leaders look like? First Thessalonians 5:12–13 is one passage that provides some answers for us. There Paul says, "We request of you, brethren, that you appreciate those who diligently labor among you, and have charge over you in the Lord and give you instruction, and that you esteem them very highly in love because of their work. Live in peace with one another." Pointing out some highlights from that text will help us to understand the nature of godly submission.

"Know" your leaders. The Greek word translated "appreciate" (*eidenai*) literally means "to know," and so its meaning

here could be understood in a number of different ways. Perhaps Paul simply means that we should acknowledge their authority (cf. 1 Cor. 16:18) or that we should recognize those who lead among us and give them a position commensurate with their ministry (in other words, to appoint leaders). But the NASB translation probably captures the true meaning of appreciation, as one commentator writes.

> It seems obvious that some feelings of tension and misunderstanding had arisen between the members and their leaders. The members seemingly had not appreciated or rightly understood the nature and function of their leaders. Therefore . . . they need to come to know their worth. They must not remain in ignorance concerning their leaders, but by reflection come to a full understanding of their true character and work.[4]

"Think the world of them." Paul says that we should "esteem them very highly," but that translation does not even come close to representing the full meaning of the original text. "Very highly" could be translated "abundantly out of all bounds, beyond all measure"[5] because it is a compound word that piles up three Greek prepositions for the sake of emphasis. It is also very likely that this command includes the idea of an outward show of great respect, since it follows a similar command that denotes an inward respect for leaders. So not only is Paul saying we should "think the world of them," but also that we should "treat them like kings"! If we want to actively submit to the leaders of our church, we should relate to them as we would to some great dignitary.

The question might arise, How can I think that highly of my leaders and show that much respect for them when they make so many mistakes? Or another question is, What if I don't like a particular leader? How can I respect someone I don't like? But Paul anticipates those questions by saying we should "esteem them very highly *in love because of their work.*" The motivation for submission, according to Paul, is not our personal feelings toward leaders, but the desire to obey God by loving them, and the realization of their position before the Lord. As Leon Morris explains,

> He wants them to be loved, and not thought of simply as the cold voice of authority. Love is the characteristic Christian attitude to man, and this should be shown within the church. Especially is this so in relationships like those between the rulers and the ruled, which in other groups of men are apt to be formal and distant. Christian love, *agape*, is not a matter of personal liking, . . . and it is in keeping with this that Paul expressly says that they are to esteem their rulers in love "for their work's sake." It is not a matter of personalities. It is the good of the church that is the important thing. The church cannot be expected to do its work effectively if the leaders are not being loyally supported by their fellows. It is a matter of fact that we are often slow to realize to this day that effective leadership in the church of Christ demands effective following. If we are continually critical of them that are set over us, small wonder if they are unable to perform the miracles that we demand of them. If we bear in mind "the work's sake" we may be more inclined to esteem them very highly in love.[6]

Don't fight with them. Paul closes his admonitions regarding our submission to leaders with the command, "Live in peace with one another." Peace is the absence of conflict, of course, and it is something both leaders and members must work hard to maintain if the church is to glorify God. The absence of conflict is not synonymous with agreement, however.

We can disagree with our leaders on various issues without creating conflict, as long as we hold our opinions with a godly humility and graciousness (cf. Prov. 18:2; 19:27; Eph. 4:15; Col. 4:6). That kind of attitude says, "At this point I don't agree with your view on this matter, but I respect you and I want to understand your thinking better."

Believe it or not, we may even be able to *disobey* without creating conflict. There may be some room for interpretation on some rulings of the church, and if we explain that we cannot go along with them because conscience dictates otherwise, the leaders may allow for an exception.

Jay Adams summarizes these ideas well.

> Only after great care and willingness to be taught and corrected by the leadership after they explain the Word of God to him, may [a member] refuse to submit to them. And then may he do so only if he is thoroughly convinced of their failure to base their case upon the Scriptures. He may not refuse to submit to authority because of personal differences or because of conflicts of any other sort. He must remember always that the authority to which he submits is not theirs but rather is the authority of Christ. . . .
>
> Even in those rare instances in which he may find himself basically at odds with the leadership of the Church, a member must be careful about the *manner* in which he differs. He may not do so in a rebellious or independent spirit. Such differences must be stated in a spirit of sorrow and with a willingness to work toward biblical agreement (Philippians 4:2: "be of one mind in the Lord").[7]

For example, a case could arise where a Sunday school teacher believes with scriptural conviction that the materials he has been asked to use are in error and dangerous to those he teaches. He should share his concerns with the leadership of the church and seek to help them understand the issues better. Perhaps they will see the danger and discontinue the use of those materials. But if they do not, then a spirit of gentleness and humility on the part of all involved should bring about a resolution that does not cause division in the body. The teacher could skip or modify those sections in the material with the permission of the leaders, or he could find another place to serve in which his conscience would not be burdened.

Sadly, some Christians have tremendous difficulty exhibiting a godly attitude when they disagree with others in the church. Proving they are right is more important to them than unity in the body, and so they wield their superior "wisdom" and "understanding" like a sledgehammer against their "foes." James 3:13–18 was written to such people.

> Who among you is wise and understanding? Let him show by his good behavior his deeds in the gentleness of wisdom. But if you have bitter jealousy and selfish ambition in your heart, do not be arrogant and so lie against the truth. This wisdom is not that which comes down from above, but is earthly, natural, demonic. For where jealousy and selfish ambition exist, there is disorder and every evil thing. But the wisdom from above is first pure, then peaceable, gentle, reasonable, full of mercy and good fruits, unwavering, without hypocrisy. And the seed whose fruit is righteousness is sown in peace by those who make peace.

The Importance of Authority in the Church

As the writer of Hebrews continues his brief discussion of our need to recognize the authority of our leaders, he pauses to explain why this authority is so necessary. He says you should obey and submit to them because "they keep watch over your souls, as those who will give an account." The imagery behind this statement probably comes from Ezekiel 3:16–21, where God called the prophet a "watchman to the house of Israel." If Ezekiel spoke the Word of the Lord to the people, he was absolved of any responsibility in their wrongdoing; but if he failed to warn them about their sin, he would be punished himself. Or as God said to the prophet, regarding a man who had not been warned, "His blood I will require at your hand."

That imagery underscores the grave responsibility God has entrusted to the leaders of a church, but it also reveals the tremendous necessity of their ministry. Individual believers, like "the house of Israel," are in need of watchmen to warn us of the encroaching enemies of the soul that would wage war against our purity or rob us of our joy. We often fail to see those enemies coming, but our leaders, who are better equipped than we are, can help us to recognize their presence and fight them more effectively. Those enemies could include false teaching, bad choices, and broken relationships. Church leaders have been ordained and gifted by God to battle such evils on our behalf (cf. Eph. 4:11–14; Gal. 6:1–6; Matt. 18:15–17).

HELPING LEADERS TO ENJOY THEIR MINISTRY

Many Christians are familiar to some extent with the first two commands in Hebrews 13:17 (to obey and submit to leaders), but few are acquainted with the third command. The writer says, in regard to our leaders' ministry of watching over our souls, "Let them do this with joy and not with grief." The idea in that command, especially in light of the Greek grammar, is that our relationship to leaders should enable them to truly enjoy their role in the body.[8]

How to Bring Them Joy

Certain activities of church members are guaranteed to bring joy to the heart of any sincere leader. Following is a list that is by no means exhaustive but may prove helpful for those who want to fulfill this important command for the glory of God and the good of the church.

Believe in Christ. Any church leader who realizes the unfortunate but inevitable presence of tares among the wheat (Matt. 13:36–42) will long and pray for the true conversion of his entire flock. He would love to know that everyone who professes Christ also possesses Christ (cf. Matt. 7:21–23), and would thrill to hear of any changes in members' lives regarding their own salvation or their doctrine of salvation. Robert Murray McCheyne once wrote,

> As I was walking in the fields, the thought came over me with almost overwhelming power that every one of my flock must soon be in heaven or hell. Oh, how I wished that I had a tongue like thunder that I might make all hear; or that I had a frame like iron that I might visit every one and say, "Escape for thy life!" Ah, sinners! you little know how I fear that you will lay the blame of your damnation at my door.[9]

Paul asked the Thessalonians, "Who is our hope or joy or crown of exultation? Is it not even you, in the presence of our Lord Jesus at His coming? For you are our glory and joy" (1 Thess. 2:19–20).

Walk in obedience to Christ. The apostle John wrote to his friend and disciple Gaius, "I was very glad when brethren came and bore witness to your truth, that is, how you are walking in truth. *I have no greater joy than this*, to hear of my children walking in the truth" (3 John 3–4). Paul expressed similar thoughts to his spiritual sons and daughters at Thessalonica.

> Now that Timothy has come to us from you, and has brought us good news of your faith and love, and that you always think kindly of us, longing to see us just as we also long to see you, for this reason, brethren, in all our distress and affliction we were comforted about you through your faith; for now we really live, if you stand firm in the Lord. For what thanks can we render to God for you in return for all the joy with which we rejoice before our God on your account. (1 Thess. 3:6–9; cf. 2 Cor. 2:3, 7:4)

Cultivate and preserve unity in the body. Paul also said to the Philippians, "If therefore there is any encouragement in Christ, if there is any consolation of love, if there is any fellowship of the Spirit, if any affection and compassion, *make my joy complete* by being of the same mind, maintaining the same love, united in spirit, intent on one purpose" (Phil. 2:1–2). He commended Philemon for being an example of a true "peacemaker" (cf. Matt. 5:9) by saying, "I thank my God always, making mention of you in my prayers, because I hear of your love, and of the faith which you have toward the Lord Jesus, and toward all the saints; . . . For I have come to have much joy and comfort in your love, because the hearts of the saints have been refreshed through you, brother" (Philem. 4–7).

Pray for them. As Aaron and Hur held up Moses' hands so that he could effectively minister to the people of Israel (Ex. 17:12), so we can support our leaders by petitioning God on their behalf. In 2 Corinthians 1:10–11 Paul wrote, "[God] will yet deliver us, you also joining in helping us through your prayers, that thanks may be given by many persons on our behalf for the favor bestowed upon us through the prayers of many."

Express personal love and loyalty to them. In that last passage, Paul is also rejoicing because of the affection the Thessalonians had expressed for him personally. That theme appears frequently in his writings, such as in 2 Corinthians 7:5–7, where he says,

> When we came into Macedonia our flesh had no rest, but we were afflicted on every side: conflicts without, fears within. But God, who comforts the depressed, comforted us by the coming of Titus; and not only by his coming, but also by the comfort with which he was comforted in you, as he reported to us your longing, your mourning, your zeal for me; so that I rejoiced even more.

Later in the same chapter he repeats the fact that both he and Titus received great comfort and joy from the affection of the Corinthians (vv. 13–16).

Seek their counsel and direction. Most leaders would like nothing more than to provide timely advice or accountability to their people, but many also battle the frustration of not knowing what is happening in our lives. We need to make an effort to share our growth and struggles with them and give them opportunities to exercise their gifts more fully. A specific question that will serve that purpose and more is, "How do you think I can better serve you and the church?"

Receive their reproof with gratefulness. Proverbs 9:8 says, "Do not reprove a scoffer, lest he hate you; reprove a wise man, and he will love you." Wise sheep will love the shepherd who rescues them when they wander from the fold, knowing that the Great Shepherd Himself chastens His flock (Heb. 12:5–11). John Brown wrote this about men in his position:

> He may urge on you unpalatable truth—he may utter sharp reproofs; but recollect he has no choice; remember he is "a man under authority." Put the question, Has he said anything that Christ has not said? If he has, disregard him; if he has not, blame him not,—he has but discharged his duty to his Master and to you; and recollect, you cannot in this case disregard the servant without doing dishonor to the Master. If he had been appointed to amuse you, to "speak smooth things" to you, you might reasonably find fault with him for his uncompromising statements and his keen rebukes. But he "watches for your souls." Your spiritual improvement, your everlasting salvation, is his object; and therefore he must not, to spare your feelings, endanger your souls. It [would be] a cruel kindness in the physician, [in order] to save a little present pain, to allow a fatal disease to fix its roots in the constitution, which must by and by produce far more suffering than what is now avoided, and not only suffering, but death.[10]

Believe the best about their character and decisions. Though we are always prone to give ourselves "the benefit of the doubt," our sinful flesh has a strong tendency to be suspicious, skeptical, and even cynical toward others. This is especially true of church leaders. Many members make a regular habit of enjoying "roast preacher" at their Sunday meal, and labels like "power trip" are often carelessly tossed around when difficult decisions are made by leadership. But biblical love, according to 1 Corinthians 13:7, "believes all things, hopes all things." A loving member will assume the best about his leaders and trust them until some clear words or actions cause him legitimate concern about their wisdom or motives. And if that happens, he will approach them humbly with the expectation that they will have a good explanation or will change in response to the loving concern.

A good member will also refuse to advance or even accept gossip about his leaders. First Timothy 5:19 says, "Do not receive an accusation against an elder except on the basis of two or three witnesses." Our natural skepticism should not be directed toward our leaders, but toward those who would accuse or slander them in any way.

Work beside them in ministry. Probably the greatest way we can bring joy to our leaders is by laboring diligently in the Lord's service, so that they do not feel a pressure to maintain and edify the church all by themselves. Their job, according to Ephesians 4:12, is to be "the equipping of the saints for the work of service ["the ministry," KJV], to the building up of the body of Christ." Therefore, it is not biblically correct to refer only to church leaders as ministers. Actually they are to be ministers to the ministers—who are the members of the church. As Jay Adams comments,

> To each member of the flock, Christ has given gifts through His Spirit and has assigned them tasks to do that are appropriate to those gifts. He has provided leadership for the purpose of helping every sheep to discover, develop and deploy his gifts in ways that contribute to the welfare of the entire flock and that further His purposes in this world. And in accordance with the abilities granted and the leadership requisite for their proper exercise, He has given each member authority to minister in His name.[11]

This multifaceted ministry of the members should include teaching (Acts 5:28; Col. 3:16–17), counseling (Rom. 15:14), "visitation" (Acts 2:46; James 1:27), administration (Acts 6:1–6), and all the "one anothers" of the New Testament. It will include generous giving, of course, so that the needs of leaders who are supported by the church can be met (cf. 1 Cor. 9:6–14; 1 Tim. 5:17–18). And it should also include their involvement in leadership itself, through helpful suggestions and even constructive criticisms designed to help the church function in a biblical and orderly manner.

How to Bring Them Grief

Hebrews 13:17 says we should help our leaders to watch over our souls with joy and "not with grief." The Greek word for "grief" literally means "groaning." Unfortunately, causing our leaders to groan in disappointment is a very real danger because of our sinful tendency to focus on ourselves rather than others. We can make their ministry difficult and unenjoyable, of course, by doing the opposite of the activities listed above.

- We grieve our leaders when we are indifferent about salvation and fail to examine ourselves regularly to see whether we are in the faith (2 Cor. 13:5).
- We grieve them when we sin against Christ or fail to grow in Him as we should.
- We grieve them when we "bite and devour one another" (Gal. 5:15) and sow discord among the brethren (Prov. 6:19).
- We grieve them when we make no effort to affirm our love for them or even know them personally.
- We grieve them when we seek counsel merely among friends or outside the church—especially when we do so in the realm of the ungodly (Ps. 1:1).

- We grieve them when we respond to their loving reproof with insults or callousness (Prov. 9:7).
- We grieve them when we distrust their motives and judge them unfairly or too hastily (1 Cor. 4:1–5).
- And finally, we grieve them by being "pew potatoes" who think our only responsibility for involvement in the church is to warm a seat on Sunday morning.

The history of God's people is sadly filled with examples of grieving leaders. Throughout the books of Exodus and Numbers, Moses was repeatedly disappointed by the stubbornness and griping of the Israelites. Even his most glorious moment as the Lord's servant—when he received the Law from God's own hand on Mount Sinai—was ruined by his return to an immoral and idolatrous people who were worshipping a golden calf. The grief and rage at his people's sin flared so violently within him that he threw the tablets down, shattering on the rocks at the foot of the mountain the greatest gift he had ever received.

Undoubtedly, the most poignant example of a grieving leader was Jeremiah. He has become known as the "weeping prophet," because he wrote an entire book of "Lamentations" and because he spent most of his life smitten by sorrow over the spiritual state of his people. The following are some passages describing his grief:

My soul, my soul! I am in anguish! Oh, my heart! My heart is pounding in me. (Jer. 4:19)

My sorrow is beyond healing, my heart is faint within me! (Jer. 8:18)

For the brokenness of the daughter of my people I am broken; I mourn, dismay has taken hold of me. (Jer. 8:21)

O, that my head were waters, and my eyes a fountain of tears, that I might weep day and night for the slain of the daughter of my people! (Jer. 9:1)

My eyes run down with streams of water because of the destruction of the daughter of my people. My eyes pour down unceasingly, without stopping, until the Lord looks down and sees from heaven. My eyes bring pain to my soul because of all the daughters of my city. (Lam. 3:48–51)

Jeremiah's intense sorrow was caused by the unbelief and disobedience of Israel, of course. More particularly, however, it was also caused by the fact that they never responded to his teaching, counsel, and reproof, even though he had been ordained and appointed by the Lord to lead them in those ways (Jer. 1).

May you never bring such sorrow to the hearts of your leaders, for the writer of Hebrews tells us that "this would be unprofitable for you." He uses a commercial Greek word for "unprofitable," echoing the same type of terminology he used when he said our leaders "will give an account." So his point is that if we do not relate to our leaders in a manner pleasing to God, we will suffer along with them. He could have said, "You're only hurting yourselves." Or as one commentator wrote, "Should they make the work and life of the leaders difficult, they would be the losers."[12]

Through God's grace, we can be winners in regard to our relationship with church leaders, and we can help them to win the race to which they have been called (1 Cor. 9:26–27). Peter says to those leaders who run the race well,

"When the Chief Shepherd appears, you will receive the unfading crown of glory" (1 Peter 5:4). But then he goes on in the next verse to address the members of a church: "You younger men, likewise, be subject to your elders; and *all of you*, clothe yourselves with humility toward one another, for God is opposed to the proud, but gives grace to the humble" (1 Peter 5:5).

QUESTIONS FOR DISCUSSION AND APPLICATION

1. Why is it important to have some kind of authority in the local church? What about in the family, at work, and in society as a whole?

2. Do you know the leaders of your church personally? How well? If you do not know them well, what are some ways you can get better acquainted with them?

3. Do you know what the vision and goals of your church leaders are? Well enough to explain it to someone who visits the church? What would you say to someone who asked what your church is trying to accomplish?

4. Ask your church leaders about their vision and goals for the coming years, and how you could help them to achieve those goals.

5

FULFILLING OUR ROLES
AS MEN AND WOMEN

A recent issue of *Time* magazine featured several articles documenting how scientific research has indicated that men and women are naturally different from one another. The lead article included these observations:

> Many scientists rely on elaborately complex and costly equipment to probe the mysteries confronting humankind. Not Melissa Hines. The UCLA behavioral scientist is hoping to solve one of life's oldest riddles with a toybox full of police cars, Lincoln Logs, and Barbie dolls. . . . Hines and her colleagues have tried to determine the origins of gender differences by capturing on videotape the squeals of delight, furrows of concentration and myriad decisions that children from 2 1/2 to 8 make while playing. Although both sexes play with all the toys available in Hines' laboratory, her work confirms what most parents (and more than a few aunts, uncles and nursery-school teachers) already know. As a group, the boys favor sports cars, fire trucks, and Lincoln Logs, while the girls are drawn more often to dolls and kitchen toys. . . .
>
> During the feminist revolution of the 1970s, talk of inborn differences in the behavior of men and women was

distinctly unfashionable, even taboo. . . . Once sexism was abolished, so the argument ran, the world would become a perfectly equitable, androgynous place, aside from a few anatomical details. But biology has a funny way of confounding expectations. Rather than disappear, the evidence for innate sexual differences only began to mount. . . .

Another generation of parents discovered that, despite their best efforts to give baseballs to their daughters and sewing kits to their sons, girls still flocked to dollhouses while boys clambered into tree forts.[1]

The cover of that magazine reads, "Why Are Men and Women Different? It isn't just upbringing. New studies show they are born that way." From the Holy Scriptures we know that is true, and we also know that the reason we are born different is that *God designed us that way* so we could fulfill different roles in His plan. Therefore, if we as Christian men and women want to please God with our full potential, particularly in the arena of the local church, we must understand the unique functions for which we have been designed.

This chapter will focus on the callings that are especially emphasized in Scripture for men and for women, rather than the responsibilities shared by both. It will also focus primarily on their roles in the church, rather than in the home or in society. Because the church and the relationships within it are a representation of God's character to the watching world (cf. Matt. 5:13–16; 1 Cor. 14:23–25; Eph. 3:10), it is essential for the witness of any congregation that men and women fulfill their designated roles.

Further, if God's will regarding men's and women's roles is ignored or misrepresented in any particular body of believers, that church simply cannot claim to be honoring Him, regardless of whatever other qualities it may boast. After speaking clearly (and probably unpopularly) to the conduct of women in the church gatherings, the apostle Paul said this to the Corinthians: "If anyone thinks he is a prophet or spiritual, let him recognize that the things which I write to you are the Lord's commandment. But if anyone does not recognize this, he is not recognized" (1 Cor. 14:37–38). In order for us to be recognized by God as obedient members of His church, we must recognize the biblical roles of men and women, fulfill them in our own lives, and help others to achieve greater conformity to them.

THE ROLE OF MEN IN THE CHURCH

Many times throughout the history of His people, God has been pictured as seeking men to fulfill the roles He has designed for them:

> The Lord has sought out for Himself a man after His own heart. (1 Sam. 13:14)

> Roam to and fro through the streets of Jerusalem, and look now, and take note. And seek in her open squares, if you can find a man, if there is one who does justice, who seeks truth, then I will pardon her. (Jer. 5:1)

> I searched for a man among them who should build up the wall and stand in the gap before Me for the land, that I should not destroy it; but I found no one. (Ezek. 22:30)

Those verses and many other similar ones indicate that it is not an overstatement to say that the welfare of God's people rises and falls on the men among them. And as the last verse indicates, the unfortunate absence of men who "stand in the gap" is all too common. Today's churches will rise to the standards of their Lord only if they have men who are loving leaders, effective teachers, and godly examples.

Loving Leaders

Leadership over the entire church is a role that has been designed especially for men. In the two-thousand-year history of Israel recorded in the Old Testament, all ongoing leadership positions (like priests, kings, and the prophets who wrote Scripture) were filled by men.[2] When Jesus began His church in the first century, all the apostles, pastors, and elders were men, and the New Testament prohibits women from serving in those positions (1 Tim. 2:11–14). They are doing so in many churches today as a result of liberal theology, the modern feminist movement, and some creative new interpretations of the biblical passages about women's roles. But for the past nineteen centuries, the orthodox church was unified in upholding the scriptural standard of male leadership.[3]

One of the reasons that an unbiblical perspective on women in leadership has gained so much persuasiveness is that so few men are stepping up to take the reins of the church and steer it in a godly direction. Christian men today need to hear the words of 1 Timothy 3:1 more than ever before: "It is a trustworthy statement: if any man aspires to the office of overseer, it is a fine work he desires to do." (That verse refers specifically to the office of overseer, or elder, but the principles in it apply to all forms of leadership that men can be involved in among the church.)

Paul begins the verse by saying that what follows "is a trustworthy statement." He uses those same words four other times in the pastoral epistles (1 Tim. 1:15; 4:9; 2 Tim. 2:11; Titus 3:8), and each time they introduce sayings that were probably quoted commonly among the early

Christians. The significance of this is explained well by Alexander Strauch in his excellent book *Biblical Eldership*:

> This expression both emphasizes and makes a positive judgment, or commendation, of the statement it is associated with. In effect, it says that what is stated is indeed true and reliable—a tried and time-proven truth that can be counted on and is fully endorsed by all believers and Paul the apostle through the Holy Spirit.
>
> The saying, . . . then, is absolutely and uncontestably true, totally reliable, and completely trustworthy. It is a truth that God's Spirit has sovereignly placed in Holy Scripture for everyone's profit. It is a truth that deserves constant repeating among the Lord's people. . . .
>
> The fact that the early Christians were prompted to create a special saying about church oversight reveals that they keenly understood the great value of overseers, the difficulties and sacrifices facing the overseers, and their own need for such leaders.[4]

Paul bolsters his encouragement for men to desire roles of leadership by saying, "It is a fine work he desires to do." Perhaps some men who read this verse may hesitate to have that desire or seek a leadership role because they think it might be selfish or sinfully ambitious to do so. Some readers may even wonder why Paul would encourage men to seek leadership, considering that our sinful nature drives us to want the top rung of the ladder and often causes us to step on others to get there.

The answer lies in the cultural situation of Paul's day and in the biblical descriptions of a leader's role. First, leadership in the early church was not always a glamorous position; persecution of Christians was rampant, and the leaders were the first to be singled out for it by the Jewish and Roman authorities (Acts 12:1–3). Second, those men who held leadership positions were commanded by Jesus Christ Himself to be servants of all (Mark 9:35; Luke 22:24–27). They were required to be loving leaders and prohibited from being authoritarian tyrants or seeking their own benefit in any way (1 Peter 5:1–3). It is that kind of leadership that Paul was encouraging each man to desire, because the welfare of the church is so utterly dependent upon it.

Christian man, have you thought and prayed carefully and earnestly about the possibility of serving the Lord and His church in this way? Are you developing your leadership skills in your personal life and in your home with the hope that God could use them for His glory in a local body of believers? You should be ready and willing to be the man that God is seeking to fulfill this crucial role, for without such men the church can only flounder spiritually and disappoint its Lord.

Effective Teachers

The role of teaching the Word of God to all the people of God is also one that has been reserved primarily for men. Although God's plan includes women communicating the principles of His Word to children and other women (Prov. 1:8; Titus 2:3–5), He has ordained that men alone should feed the whole flock of God when it gathers (1 Tim. 2:12–14; 1 Cor. 14:34–35). Unfortunately, as in the area of leadership, there is often a lack of men willing and able to fulfill this role, and that sad fact has contributed to the growing number of women in teaching positions. If churches want to stem the tide of this reversal of biblical roles, it will not be enough simply to emphasize the restrictions placed on women in ministry—they will also have to emphasize the need for men to develop their teaching abilities.

One reason for the shortage of male teachers today may be the common idea that Bible teaching is the responsibility of pastors and elders alone. Many "laymen" never even consider whether they are gifted to teach because they think they would have to attend seminary to do so. The same basic problem exists in regard to counseling, which requires teaching skills to be successful. But, although formal training does yield considerable benefits and church offices do need to be filled with men who are especially qualified, it is impossible in most churches for the staff and elders alone to carry out all the ministries of teaching the Word and counseling fully and effectively. Those church leaders need other men in the church to be partners in those ministries.

Every man in the church should be intentionally developing and practicing his teaching skills, because every man is at least a husband or potential husband, and God has commanded husbands to be teachers in the home (Deut. 6:6–7; Eph. 5:25–27; 6:4). The key to doing that lies in exciting personal Bible study, because when we learn profound truths from God's Word personally and apply them in our own lives, a desire will grow to share them with others. It is when the word of Christ dwells in us richly that we will find ourselves teaching and admonishing one another (Col. 3:16).

Godly Examples

Although every member of the body of Christ is commanded to be a godly example that leads others to grow in Christ, the men of the church are especially commissioned to serve others in this way. Being an example is such an integral part of effective leading and teaching that those roles cannot be fulfilled effectively without it (1 Peter 5:3; 2 Thess. 3:6–7). Also, husbands are called by God to relate to their wives in a way that typifies the Great Example, Jesus Christ (Eph. 5:25–27).

First Timothy 3:2–13 and Titus 1:6–9 contain lists of character traits that are true of a godly man. The primary purpose of those lists is to identify which men may serve in the church offices of elder and deacon, but a secondary purpose is to challenge every man in the church to cultivate those traits in his life. We know that because Paul encourages any man who desires the church offices (1 Tim. 3:1, 13). Moreover, none of the qualifications in the lists is too high for any man to attain through God's gracious enabling. Actually, the characteristics listed are simply those which should be true of every Christian man (in some growing degree), and Paul is saying that we should not appoint to leadership anyone who lacks one or more of them.

Below are the twenty-five qualities mentioned in regard to elders and deacons. This is not meant to be an exhaustive discussion of the interpretive issues and practical ramifications of these qualities, but merely a brief explanation of each one, designed to help men evaluate the example they are presenting to others in the church.[5]

"Above reproach" (probably a general heading for the other qualities) means that I live a consistent life of growth in godliness over an extended period of time so that no one can legitimately question my salvation, sanctification, or sincerity.

"Husband of one wife" (or "one-woman man") means that I consistently express affection and devotion to my wife and not to other women. If I am single, it means that I practice sexual purity in mind and action.

"Temperate" means that I am sober, careful, and controlled in my actions. I do not indulge in food, drink, or any pleasure beyond the limits of Scripture, conscience, or good sense.

"Prudent" (also translated "sensible") means that I am sober, careful, and control my thinking according to God's

Word. I am not subject to whims of thought or emotions, nor do I accept my own ideas or the ideas of others without biblical scrutiny.

"Respectable" (or "orderly") means that I live an organized and structured life in which I plan to make the wisest use of my time and can be depended upon to fulfill both big and small responsibilities.

"Hospitable" (lit. "a friend of strangers") means that my home and other possessions belong to God rather than me, and I am willing and ready to share them even with those who may never do anything for me.

"Able to teach" means that I have learned enough biblical doctrine from my own study and from faithful teachers that I can instruct others accurately and effectively.

"Not addicted to wine" means that I could never be considered as someone whose judgment is impaired by the use of alcohol or other substances.

"Not pugnacious" means that I never resort to any form of physical or verbal violence in my relationships with family, friends, acquaintances, or even enemies.

"Gentle" means that I respond to others' shortcomings, and even their abuse, with loving concern rather than hurtful comments or any other kind of retaliation.

"Uncontentious" means that the last thing I want to do is enter into a debate or conflict, though I know they will arise at times. I have repeatedly shown the ability to disagree with others without creating division in the body.

"Free from the love of money" means that my motivations in my work and investments is never to get rich or even accrue more possessions for myself. I view the money I make merely as a means to fulfill the scriptural duties of providing for myself and my family, supporting God's work, and giving to those in need.

"Manages his household well" means that I fulfill the role of a godly leader in my home in regard to whatever responsibilities God has given me there. If I have children, I must be such a good leader, example, discipler, and discipliner that they lead obedient and exemplary lives.

"Not a new convert" means that I will take pains to grow as fast as I can in Christ so that others can view me as spiritually mature. I also will be careful to cultivate humility in my life so that I do not fall into the pit of spiritual pride.

"A good reputation with those outside the church" means that my conduct does not change when I leave the company of Christians; I am as conscientious, honest, and caring when I work, drive, and shop as I am when I am teaching a Sunday school class.

"Men of dignity" means that I am serious enough that no one could accuse me of being frivolous or not recognizing the gravity of spiritual matters.

"Not double-tongued" means that I do not say one thing to one person and the opposite to someone else. I also do not speak freely when something is better left unsaid.

"Holding to the mystery of the faith with a clear conscience" means that I understand biblical doctrine, but I also live it to such an extent that I have no unconfessed sin or doubts about the righteousness of any activity in my life.

"Not self-willed" means that I consider myself as less important than others and seek their good above my own.

"Not quick-tempered" means that I do not "blow up" when I am mistreated or things do not go my way. I do not act a certain way in the heat of the moment that I have to regret later.

"Loving what is good" means that I rejoice in my own obedience and growth and the obedience and growth of others, so much so that I will gladly do whatever I can to facilitate that growth.

"Just" means that I do not show partiality to one kind of person over another, and that I can be counted on to act in a consistently biblical manner in my dealings with others.

"Devout" means that I constantly worship God by setting myself apart from sin and the encumbrances that could tempt me to sin.

"Self-controlled" means that I have developed the habit of fighting and overcoming my sinful desires rather than giving in to them. I practice personal discipline even in nonmoral matters so that I may be better equipped to defeat temptation when it arises.

"Holding fast the faithful word" means that I study Scripture in enough depth to be able to "hold my own" in a conversation with a heretic or misled brother.

These divine standards for men are admittedly high—but again it must be emphasized that we all are capable of being the kind of examples described in those passages (through the power of the Holy Spirit). It seems that many men in the body of Christ have considered those qualifications to apply only to elders and deacons, and therefore they have not made it a priority to bring their own lives up to God's standard. May God grant His church more and more men who will pursue the role of loving leader, effective teacher, and godly example.

THE ROLE OF WOMEN IN THE CHURCH

The last few decades in America have brought tremendous changes in women's involvement in church ministry, as the book *Megatrends for Women* attests in a chapter entitled "To Hell With Sexism: Women in Religion":

> Women of the late 20th century are revolutionizing the most sexist institution in history—organized religion. Overturning

millennia of tradition, they are challenging authorities, rein-
terpreting the Bible, creating their own services, crowding into
seminaries, winning the right to ordination, purging sexist
language in liturgy, re-integrating female values and assuming positions of leadership.[6]

Among the "Christian feminists" who support these developments, one of the most common allegations against traditional views of the woman's role is that they are "sexist,"
or in other words, demeaning to women. That accusation,
however, is a "straw man," a caricature. Traditional views that
are rooted in biblical doctrines have in fact been used by God
throughout history to *improve* respect for women, not op-
press them.

Women were esteemed and lauded in ancient Israel in
a manner not shared by most of the other societies of the
time. The nation's law demanded the atypical practice of
monogamous marriage (cf. Prov. 5:15–21), and God sent
judgment upon any man who was unfaithful to the wife of
his youth (1 Kings 11; Mal. 2:13–16). The book of Proverbs
says that "an excellent wife is the crown of her husband"
(12:4) and that "her worth is far above jewels" (31:10).

In New Testament times, Paul's command that husbands
should love their wives as their own bodies (Eph. 5:28–30) was
nothing short of revolutionary to the citizens of a Greco-Roman
culture, where a man's wife was his maid and numerous con-
cubines were his sexual partners. And even in the late Puritan
age of our country, immediately following a time when the prevailing religious attitudes were the most conservative ever, women
were spared disgrace of every kind. As one historian writes,

When Philip Schaff wrote back to his learned friends in
Germany in 1855, trying to explain to them what America

was like, he said that "America's profound respect for the female sex is well known." Indeed, he said, America is "sometimes called woman's paradise" because the woman was spared the hard drudgery common in Europe, was so regarded by men as to be able to travel freely without molestation, and "she has the precedence in every company." In Europe, a speaker addressing a mixed crowd would begin, "Gentlemen and Ladies"; in America, speakers addressing the same crowd would say, "Ladies and Gentlemen."[7]

Biblical Christians recognize that God's Word clearly places some restrictions on the ministries of women in the church. We do not believe God made women inferior to men, however, but that He simply made them *different* from men. Just as each of the parts of an engine must accomplish a distinct task to make the car run smoothly, and just as every player on a team must play a unique role in order for it to win, so men and women must perform different functions in the church in order for it to honor God.

Some of the main parts God has designed for a woman to play in His body are those of a submissive learner, a gifted trainer, a skilled hostess, and a humble servant.

Submissive Learners

Although every member of the body of Christ is commanded to be submissive to others (Eph. 5:21), Scripture especially emphasizes this trait when speaking of the roles of women. Consider the following passages, which all have special reference to the conduct of women in the public gatherings of the church:

> I want you to understand that Christ is the head of every man, and the man is the head of a woman, and God is the head of Christ. . . . a man ought not to have his head

covered, since he is the image and glory of God; but the woman is the glory of man. For man does not originate from woman, but woman from man; for indeed man was not created for the woman's sake, but woman for the man's sake. Therefore the woman ought to have a symbol of authority on her head. (1 Cor. 11:3–10)

Let the women keep silent in the churches; for they are not permitted to speak, but let them subject themselves, just as the Law also says. And if they desire to learn anything, let them ask their own husbands at home; for it is improper for a woman to speak in church. Was it from you that the word of God first went forth? Or has it come to you only? If anyone thinks he is a prophet or spiritual, let him recognize that the things which I write to you are the Lord's commandment. But if anyone does not recognize this, he is not recognized. (1 Cor. 14:34–38)

Let a woman quietly receive instruction with entire submissiveness. But I do not allow a woman to teach or exercise authority over a man, but to remain quiet. For it was Adam who was first created, and then Eve. And it was not Adam who was deceived, but the woman being quite deceived, fell into transgression. (1 Tim. 2:11–14)

The numerous interpretive issues in these passages and the many questions of application that arise from them are beyond the scope of our discussion in this chapter. They are dealt with ably and exhaustively elsewhere.[8] But two concepts are very clear in those passages and are not legitimately open to interpretation: (1) In the context of the local church, each woman should submit herself to male leadership and should learn from the teaching of men rather than being a teacher of men. (2) Eldership and other positions of authority over men are not a biblical option for a Christian woman, nor is any kind of teaching or counseling role in which she would be exercising authority over men. God has designed for the submissive learning of women to be a key element in the revelation of His character through the church and the effective witness of the body.

Again, this submissive role of women does not mean that they are inferior to men in any way. The difference between men and women is not one of quality or ability, but of function. This difference is illustrated in 1 Corinthians 11:3, where Paul says, "I want you to understand that Christ is the head of every man, and the man is the head of a woman, and God is the head of Christ." Man being the head of the woman does not mean man is superior to woman any more than God's being the head of Christ means that God is superior to Christ! "God is the head of Christ" refers to the subservient role Jesus took upon Himself when He walked the earth, and "man is the head of woman" simply refers to the differing roles God has assigned to men and women.

And the "differing role" of women, contrary to the complaints of feminists, is not a burdensome one at all. As William Hendriksen wrote in his commentary on 1 Timothy,

> Though these words in I Timothy 2:11 and 12 and their parallel in I Corinthians 14:33–35 may sound a trifle unfriendly, in reality, they are the very opposite. In fact, they are expressive of the feeling of tender sympathy and basic understanding. They mean: let a woman not enter a sphere of activity for which by dint of her very creation she is not suited. Let not a bird try to dwell under water. Let not a fish try to live on land. Let not a woman try to exercise authority over a man by lecturing him in public worship. For the sake both

109

of herself and the spiritual welfare of the church such unholy tampering with the divine authority is forbidden.[9]

In a similar vein, R. L. Dabney wrote,

Paul does not say that the woman must not preach in public because he regards her as less pious, less zealous, less
eloquent, less learned, less brave or less intellectual than
man. In the advocates of women's right to this function
there is a continual tendency to a confusion of thought, as
though the apostle, when he says that a woman must not
do what a man does, meant to disparage her sex. This is a
sheer mistake . . . woman is excluded from this masculine
task of public preaching by Paul, not because she is inferior to man, but simply because her Maker has ordained
her for another work which is incompatible with this. So he
might have pronounced, as nature does, that she shall not
sing bass, not because he thought the bass chords more
beautiful—perhaps he thought the pure alto of the femi-
nine throat far sweeter—but because her very constitution
fits her for the latter part in the concert of human existence,
and therefore unfits her for the other, the coarser and less
melodious part.[10]

Our sinful society (and perhaps our sinful hearts) have
convinced many of us that it is more blessed to lead than it is
to follow. That is not necessarily true, for leadership brings
problems, difficulties, and heartaches that followers never experience. God made women to be dependent upon men, so
that men would protect, provide, and care for women. Any
husband who truly loves his wife and desires to be the proper
head of the home knows that this is no easy task. Sometimes
it would be much more enjoyable to follow than to lead. And
any elder who truly loves the Lord and desires to be the proper

leader of the church knows that his is no easy task. During many difficult times he might desire strongly to relinquish his role to an eager successor!

The direction and instruction of the church is not a burden that women must bear. They should be grateful to God for that, and joyfully seek to fulfill the many other crucial ministries to which they have been called.

Gifted Trainers

Women are not intended to teach men, but that does not mean they are without giftedness in the areas of discipling and training. On the contrary, they are essential instruments in God's plan for the education of children and other women.

The training of children. First Timothy 5:9–10 discusses a list of older widows kept by the early church, which was probably for the purpose of identifying those women who would commit themselves to a special position of service in the body. The requirements given for women to be placed on the list reveal the ministries that godly women can and should fulfill. She must have "a reputation for good works," and the first good work mentioned is the rearing of children. Paul says a woman can be placed on the list "if she has brought up children." The Greek word translated "brought up" is the same word used in Ephesians 6:4, which says, "Fathers [and, we may infer, "mothers"], do not provoke your children to anger; but bring them up in the discipline and instruction of the Lord." And in 1 Timothy 2:15, Paul follows his discussion of the restrictions God has placed on women in ministry by saying, "But women shall be preserved through the bearing of children if they continue in faith and love and sanctity with self-restraint."

Those verses (and others in Scripture) seem to indicate that women play a primary role in the development of children.

111

The command to be "workers at home" allows women to spend the most time with children, and in most cases they are apparently much more gifted than men for this task. At the very least, the Scripture clearly states that the woman's role in raising children is indispensable. In Exodus 20:12, the fifth commandment says, "Honor your father and your mother." In God's eyes, the mother must be honored just as much as the father. Exodus 21:15 states that "he who strikes his father or his mother shall surely be put to death." Exodus 21:17 declares, "He who curses his father or his mother shall surely be put to death." In God's eyes, despising and disobeying the mother is just as serious as despising and disobeying the father.

The book of Proverbs is replete with illustrations that admonish children to give equal respect to fathers and mothers. Proverbs 1:8 says, "Hear, my son, your father's instruction, and do not forsake your mother's teaching"; Proverbs 6:20 says, "My son, observe the commandment of your father, and do not forsake the teaching of your mother"; and Proverbs 30:17 asserts, "The eye that mocks a father, and scorns a mother, the ravens of the valley will pick it out, and the young eagles will eat it." Again and again, children are instructed to obey their mothers, just as they obey their fathers. Again and again, God says that He will punish children for disobedience to the mother even as He will punish children for disobedience to the father.

Certainly if raising children is a special ministry for women, women ought to, if possible, have children. There are times when that may be physically impossible, but when she can have children, she should have them. And when she does have them, she should "bring them up in the discipline and instruction of the Lord" so that they can greatly impact the church and the world for Christ. Think of the contribution so many women have made to the world throughout history by raising godly leaders. In a very real sense the adage "The hand that rocks the cradle rules the world" is true. Women can make a tremendous contribution to the church and the world from the bottom up instead of from the top down.

But what about the women who do not have children, or what about the women whose children have departed from the home? Can such women still have a ministry to children? Yes, because if they do not have children of their own, they should find some children and help to "bring them up." They can invite the children of others into their homes. They can have fun with these children and talk to them about the Savior. Some parents with several children are very busy, and women without children can have a tremendous influence on the lives of these children, who may need more adult supervision and attention than their parents can give.

Even women without children may have a special gift for working with children. God has given that gift to them and they should use it. Women should be seeking out the little ones and leading them to Jesus. Though parents may have often exhorted and rebuked their children with little success, sometimes the same exhortation or rebuke coming from someone else carries added weight and produces results. Women may never know the extent of their influence in the lives of children until they get to heaven, but they may be assured that their influence is great.

The training of younger women. It is so sad to hear older Christian women say things like, "I have had my children. I have brought them up, and now I am on vacation. I don't want to get involved with children now. I don't want those problems again." But God has given them tremendous wisdom about the home and raising children through their experience. At that point in their lives they should be saying, "My ministry is just beginning!"

Titus 2:3–5 says, "Older women likewise are to be . . . teaching what is good, that they may encourage the young women to love their husbands, to love their children, to be sensible, pure, workers at home, kind, being subject to their own husbands, that the word of God may not be dishonored."

Older women should be continually teaching younger women because they have had years of experience. And young women should teach the even younger women what they have learned through their searching the Scriptures and through their Christian experience. This is a key responsibility and privilege of women in the church.

Since there are more women and children in the world than men, what a mission field women have! Some women complain, "I don't have anything to do for Christ." But the women who say that usually are looking for an excuse because they do not really want to serve Christ sacrificially. Women can never legitimately say that they have nothing to do for Christ until they have taught every needy child and every needy woman in the church and in their community everything they know about the Word of God. In fact, these are ministries that women can often perform better than men, because there are problems among children and other women that women can deal with better than men. Women may disclose personal problems to other women that they would not discuss with men, and women often can understand the emotional makeup and disposition of other women better than men.

Skilled Hostesses

First Timothy 5:10 indicates another important ministry of women in the church when it says a widow can be put on the list "if she has shown hospitality to strangers." The ministry of hospitality has largely been forgotten today, but it was a key ingredient in the life of the early church. Alexander Strauch wrote an excellent little book about this issue called *Using Your Home for Christ*, which contains the following summary:

- Hospitality is a crucial element in building Christian community. Hospitality may well be the best means we have to promote close, brotherly love. It is especially important in churches where people don't know each other or where relationships are superficial, Sunday-morning-only relationships.
- Hospitality is an effective tool for evangelism. Showing Christ's love to others in a home environment may be the only means Christians have to reach their neighbors for Christ. A Christian home can be a lighthouse for God in a spiritually dark neighborhood. . . .
- Hospitality is a biblical command. Many Christians do not realize what the New Testament teaches about hospitality and what it can do for the local church.[11]

The commands he mentions are found in Romans 12:13, 1 Peter 4:9, and Hebrews 13:2. The last verse says, "Do not neglect to show hospitality to strangers, for by this some have entertained angels without knowing it." Certainly Strauch is right that the virtue of hospitality should be rediscovered, and even though men are called to be "hospitable" (1 Tim. 3:2), it is often the women in the church who are the most uniquely gifted for that ministry. They have been designed to be "workers at home," and hospitality for the purposes of edification and evangelism is a ministry that fits perfectly with their efforts in that domain.

Consider carefully the words of mother and homemaker (and seminary graduate) Dorothy Patterson:

> Women have been liberated right out of the genuine freedom they enjoyed for centuries to oversee the home, rear the children, and pursue personal creativity; they have been brainwashed to believe that the absence of a titled, payroll occupation enslaves a woman to failure, boredom, and imprisonment within the confines of home. Though feminism speaks of liberation, self-fulfillment, personal rights, and breaking down barriers, these phrases inevitably mean the opposite. In fact, the opposite is true because a salaried job and titled position can inhibit a woman's natural nesting instinct and maternity by inverting her priorities so that failures almost inevitably come in the rearing of her own children and the building of an earthly shelter for those whom she loves most. The mundane accompanies every task, however high paying or prestigious the job, so that escape from boredom is not inevitable just because your workplace is not at home. And where is the time for personal creativity when you are in essence working two jobs—one at home and one away? . . .
>
> Homemaking—being a full-time wife and mother—is not a destructive drought of usefulness but an overflowing oasis of opportunity; it is not a dreary cell to contain one's talents and skills but a brilliant catalyst to channel creativity and energies into meaningful work; it is not a rope for binding one's productivity in the marketplace, but reins for guiding one's posterity in the home; it is not repressive restraint of intellectual prowess for the community, but a release of wise instruction to your own household; it is not the bitter assignment of inferiority to your person, but the bright assurance of the ingenuity of God's plan for complementarity of the sexes, especially as worked out in God's plan for marriage; it is neither limitation of gifts available

nor stinginess in distributing the benefits of those gifts, but rather the multiplication of a mother's legacy to the generations to come and the generous bestowal of all God meant a mother to give to those entrusted to her care.[12]

Humble Servants

First Timothy 5:10 also says that a woman can be placed on the list "if she has washed the saints' feet, [and] if she has assisted those in distress." At the time of Paul, women literally washed the feet of the saints, because that ministry was needed when the church gathered. To today's church, that act represents the need for women to fulfill the role of servants by ministering to the physical needs of the church members, and even the church building. And godly women can serve very effectively by assisting those in some kind of distress, whether they be single mothers and their children, shut-ins, the infirm, or those who have financial needs (cf. 1 Tim. 5:16).

So the roles of submissive learners, gifted trainers, skilled hostesses, and humble servants are some of the functions that women can fulfill in the church. No doubt any open-minded person will realize that there is more than enough to keep a godly woman busy in her service for Christ. Any open-minded person will also realize that the tasks God has assigned to women are not insignificant, but very important. In fact, they are every bit as important as the tasks that God has assigned to the men. They are different in some respects from the tasks of men, but just because they are different doesn't mean that they are unimportant.

In Genesis 3:1, Satan said to Eve, "Indeed, has God said, 'You shall not eat from any tree of the garden'?" That was not true. God had said, "From any tree of the garden you may eat freely; but from the tree of the knowledge of good and evil you shall not eat" (Gen. 2:16–17). Satan, however, wanted to focus Eve's attention on what she could not do. And that is what Satan is doing with women today. He is suggesting to women that men are using them as their slaves and servants. He encourages them to stand up and let the men know that women have every right to do everything that men may do. He wants women to concentrate on the things they have been forbidden to do and leave undone the important tasks that they can and should accomplish.

May God help Christian women not to groan or complain about what God has not designed them to do, but instead gratefully and enthusiastically perform their God-given ministries. And may God help men to discharge their responsibilities as well, because when women and men are fulfilling the roles for which we have been designed, He will receive glory.

QUESTIONS FOR DISCUSSION AND APPLICATION

1. What are some things that men can do to prepare themselves to become leaders in the church (or better leaders)?

2. Why is it so important that men be godly examples, in the home, in the church, and in society? Discuss some examples of good and bad modeling, and the effects of each.

3. What would you say to someone who complained that differing roles in the church are demeaning to women?

4. Discuss some specific ways that women can practice hospitality and that men can encourage and support them in doing so.

6

PARTICIPATING IN WORSHIP SERVICES

Modern man worships his work, works at his play, and plays at his worship.[1]

Worship is a lost art in contemporary Christianity. Even worse, it is a forgotten duty. Many of us use the term "worship service" to describe the gathering of believers on a Sunday, but how many of us truly approach those gatherings with a singular focus on participating in worship? How many of us even understand the nature and elements of worship well enough that we could accurately evaluate whether we are worshipping in a manner that pleases God?

Every Christian *must* understand and practice biblical worship because God has repeatedly commanded us to do so (Deut. 6:13; Matt. 4:10), because true worship is a confirmation of our salvation in Christ (John 4:23–24; Phil. 3:3), and because the absence of true worship and the presence of false worship arouse the terrifying judgment of a jealous God (1 Sam. 13:8–14; Rom. 1:18–32).

Furthermore, the lives of God's people throughout all ages have been consistently characterized by worship. Hebrews

11:4, describing one of the first human beings, says, "By faith Abel offered to God a better sacrifice than Cain, through which he obtained the testimony that he was righteous, God testifying about his gifts." Immediately after the Flood, "Noah built an altar to the Lord, and took of every clean animal and of every clean bird and offered burnt offerings on the altar" (Gen. 8:20). Abraham likewise erected places of worship at every stop along his journey to the land God had promised him (Gen. 12:7–8; 13:4).

The history of Israel also reveals the emphasis God places upon worship in the lives of His people. As John MacArthur has written,

> In the Old Testament, worship covered all of life; it was the focus of the people of God. For example, the Tabernacle was designed and laid out to emphasize the priority of worship. The description of its details requires seven chapters—243 verses—in Exodus, yet only 31 verses in Genesis are devoted to the creation of the world. . . .
>
> The arrangement of the camp suggests that worship was central to all other activity. The Tabernacle was in the center, and immediately next to it were the priests, who led in the worship. A little farther out from the Tabernacle were the Levites, who were involved in service. Beyond that were all the tribes, facing toward the center, the place of worship.[2]

The tabernacle was later replaced by the temple, which also was the center of the nation's life and also required voluminous instructions for its construction and maintenance. Throughout the rest of the Old Testament, God either blessed or punished Israel based on the quality of their worship. Even its last book, Malachi, is filled with warnings that the nation would fall under the judgment of God if they did not cease their false and half-hearted worship.

Since the New Testament church has been instituted, of course, worship has remained an essential priority for the people of God. So every believer has an obligation to understand its significance and practice it continually. Our Lord Jesus Christ says to every one of us, "You shall worship the Lord your God" (Matt. 4:10).

THE ESSENCE OF CORPORATE WORSHIP

Our word "worship" is derived from the old English word "worthship," and that helps us to understand its basic meaning. Worship is acknowledging the unique worth of an object and showing honor and respect to it. So biblical words like honor, respect, awe, adoration, reverence, and glorifying are often near synonyms for the term "worship," communicating a similar idea. Obviously this practice is not one that is limited to public gatherings. In fact, in Scripture those terms are used much more often in regard to our personal relationship with God than to our activities in the presence of other Christians.

So God requires us to be involved in personal, private worship as a way of life—but He also wants us to worship Him with other believers. This corporate, public worship has always been a companion to individual, private worship, and it has always been equally necessary. It is primarily the corporate worship of the church that this chapter will discuss. Scripture teaches several principles about such worship that we must understand if we are to participate properly in it.

The focus of true worship is on God. Psalms 95 and 96 are two of the greatest passages in Scripture about corporate

121

worship. They say, "Come, let us worship and bow down; let us kneel before the LORD our Maker. For He is our God" (95:6–7); and "Ascribe to the LORD the glory of His name; bring an offering, and come into His courts. Worship the LORD in the splendor of holiness" (96:8–9). Notice how often the Lord is referred to in those brief passages. He is the sole object of worship and the dominant character in the drama of worship. The primary purpose of worship is to bring Him glory and pleasure, and so the interests and needs of men are only of secondary importance. In fact, they are important only so far as they are opportunities for God to bring more glory to Himself.

Unfortunately, we can often approach corporate worship with our focus on something other than the person and glory of God. We can think primarily about how *we* are enjoying the service, whether *we* are profiting from it—or we may even be preoccupied with matters that have nothing to do with worship. The Sunday meal, football, interpersonal relations, our appearance, and any number of trivialities can push God out from the center of our focus. But if we are to worship in a biblical manner, we must concentrate our hearts and minds on the One we are gathering to honor. Donald Whitney explains,

> The more we focus on God, the more we understand and appreciate how worthy He is. As we understand and appreciate this, we can't help but respond to Him. Just as an indescribable sunset or a breathtaking mountaintop vista evokes a spontaneous response, so we cannot encounter the worthiness of God without the response of worship. If you could see God at this moment, you would so utterly understand how worthy He is of worship that you would instinctively fall on your face and worship Him. That's why we

read in Revelation that those around the throne who see Him fall on their faces in worship and those creatures closest to Him are so astonished with His worthiness that throughout eternity they ceaselessly worship Him with the response of "Holy, holy, holy. . . ."

Since worship is focusing on and responding to God, regardless of what else we are doing we are not worshiping if we are not thinking about God. You may be listening to a sermon, but without thinking of how God's truth applies to your life and affects your relationship with Him, you aren't worshiping. You may be singing "Holy, holy, holy," but if you aren't thinking about God while singing it, you are not worshiping. You may be listening to someone pray, but if you aren't thinking of God and praying with them, you aren't worshiping."[3]

The participants in true worship actively respond to God with their whole being. True worship involves an active response to God, rather than the passive onlooking that we often associate with attending a worship service. Psalms 95 and 96 command God's people to come physically to the place of corporate worship; they speak of talking to Him, singing to Him, bowing before Him, kneeling before Him, bringing an offering, and even trembling before Him. These pictures of public worship clearly indicate that no Christian should be a "pew potato" who can easily be mistaken for part of the church furniture. God wants us to participate outwardly and physically in the service in whatever ways are appropriate.

The inward part of our being must also be eagerly and sincerely involved in public worship, however. Jesus told the woman at the well that "the true worshipers shall worship the Father *in spirit* and truth; for such people the Father seeks to be His worshipers. God is spirit, and those who worship Him must worship *in spirit* and truth" (John 4:23–24, emphasis added). We must exercise spiritual discipline to avoid becoming like those Jesus described with words from the prophet Isaiah: "This people honors Me with their lips, but their heart is far away from Me. But in vain do they worship Me" (Mark 7:6–7). John Piper illustrates this danger well.

> If God's reality is displayed to us in His Word or his world, and we do not then feel in our heart any grief or longing or hope or fear or awe or joy or gratitude or confidence, then we may dutifully sing and pray and recite and gesture as much as we like, but it will not be real worship. We cannot honor God if our "heart is far from him."
>
> Worship is a way of gladly reflecting back to God the radiance of his worth. This cannot be done by mere acts of duty. It can be done only when spontaneous affections arise in the heart.
>
> Consider the analogy of a wedding anniversary. Mine is on December 21. Suppose on this day I bring home a dozen long-stemmed red roses for Noel. When she meets me at the door I hold out the roses, and she says, "Oh, Johnny, they're beautiful, thank you," and gives me a big hug. Then suppose I hold up my hand and say matter-of-factly, "Don't mention it; it's my duty."
>
> What happens? Is not the exercise of duty a noble thing? Do not we honor those we dutifully serve? Not much. Not if there's no heart in it. Dutiful roses are a contradiction in terms. If I'm not moved by a spontaneous affection for her as a person, the roses don't honor her. In fact they belittle her. They are a very thin covering for the fact that she does not have the worth or beauty in my eyes to kindle affection. All I can muster is a calculated expression of marital duty. . . .
>
> The real duty of worship is not the outward duty to say or do the liturgy. It is the inward duty, the command—

"Delight yourself in the Lord!" (Psalm 37:4). "Be glad in the Lord and rejoice!" (Psalm 32:11).

The reason this is the real duty of worship is that this honors God, while the empty performance of ritual does not. If I take my wife out for the evening on our anniversary and she asks me, "Why do you do this?" the answer that honors her most is, "Because nothing makes me happier tonight than to be with you."

"It's my duty," is a dishonor to her.

"It's my joy," is an honor.[4]

For our worship to be fully pleasing to God, it must be motivated by joy and not merely duty. Though obedience is never less than our duty, the truest expression of worship occurs when our duty becomes our delight.

THE ELEMENTS OF CORPORATE WORSHIP

In the Scriptures not only are we informed about the nature of true worship, but we are also instructed regarding various activities that should be included in the church gatherings. A brief consideration of each of these activities will help us to understand their importance and the role individual Christians play in them.

Preparing for Public Worship

The right kind of participation in a worship service begins long before the service actually starts. Our attitudes and actions during the week will often determine whether we will be pleasing to God on Sunday.

The most important issue in this regard is whether we spend the week walking with God in holiness. In Psalm 15 David asks, "O LORD, who may abide in Thy tent? Who may dwell on Thy holy hill?" (v. 1). Even though these words refer primarily to our individual salvation and sanctification, their "sanctuary" imagery also makes them applicable to the subject of corporate worship. To the question of who is a true worshiper, God answers,

> He who walks with integrity, and works righteousness, and speaks truth in his heart. He does not slander with his tongue, nor does evil to his neighbor, nor takes up a reproach against his friend; in whose eyes a reprobate is despised, but who honors those who fear the LORD; he swears to his own hurt, and does not change; he does not put out his money at interest, nor does he take a bribe against the innocent. (vv. 2–5)

That passage clearly indicates that the quality of our worship in the church is dependent upon the integrity of our lives in the world. Hebrews 10:22 is another passage that speaks of personal holiness while using the terminology of public worship. It says, "Let us draw near with a sincere heart in full assurance of faith, having our hearts sprinkled clean from an evil conscience and our bodies washed with pure water."

Our relationships with other Christians must be right if our worship is to be acceptable to God. Matthew 5:23–24 says, "If therefore you are presenting your offering at the altar, and there remember that your brother has something against you, leave your offering there before the altar, and go your way; first be reconciled to your brother, and then come and present your offering."

We also must worship God privately during the week if we want to please Him in our public worship. In fact, many have observed that those who participate most joyfully and profitably in the worship services are those who have the most frequent and vibrant personal times with God during the week. Their worship on Sunday is an overflow of the exciting relationship they have had with God during the days before.

Praying specifically for the church services is another way of preparing ourselves for them, and so are such seemingly mundane matters as going to bed early on Saturday night and getting up early enough that we do not have to rush to church. All these things actually have tremendous importance when we realize the gravity of the spiritual responsibilities resting upon us when we gather to worship. Consider the words of Charles Spurgeon:

> There should be some preparation of the heart in coming to the worship of God. Consider who he is in whose name we gather, and surely we cannot rush together without thought. Consider whom we profess to worship, and we shall not hurry into his presence as men run to a fire. Moses, the man of God, was warned to put off his shoes from his feet when God only revealed himself in a bush. How should we prepare ourselves when we come to him who reveals himself in Christ Jesus, his dear Son? There should be no stumbling into the place of worship half asleep, no roaming here as if it were no more than going to a playhouse. We cannot expect to profit much if we bring with us a swarm of idle thoughts and a heart crammed with vanity. If we are full of folly, we may shut out the truth of God from our minds.[5]

Learning from the Teaching of God's Word

The last words of that quote from Spurgeon describe an all-too-frequent occurrence in Bible-believing churches. The Word of God is proclaimed from the pulpit, yet the listeners often learn very little from it and change very little as a result of it. That is unacceptable and displeasing to God because He has placed the teaching of His Word at the forefront of corporate worship. Biblical worship has always involved hearing from God as well as giving to Him. In fact, giving of ourselves to God is most often a *response* to the wonderful truths He communicates to us through divine revelation.

The centrality of biblical teaching in corporate worship is apparent to anyone who peruses the New Testament. The members of the early church "were continually devoting themselves to the apostles' teaching" (Acts 2:42; cf. 5:42), and it seems clear from many New Testament examples that such teaching was the prominent feature of every public service. Paul's words to Timothy regarding the local church were recorded for the sake of all the eras to come. "Give attention to the public reading of Scripture, to exhortation and teaching. . . . take pains with these things; be absorbed in them" (1 Tim. 4:13–15).

If worship services should find their greatest appeal and benefit in the revelation of God through the teaching of His Word, why does there seem to be such ineffectiveness and boredom generated by many preachers? Certainly one answer is that many men who proclaim God's Word are not trained as well as they should be and do not prepare as well as they could. Perhaps many even lack the giftedness to be effective teachers. But Jay Adams, in his excellent book *A Consumer's Guide to Preaching*, offers another explanation in addition to that one. He says that those who listen to sermons are just as much to blame for their ineffectiveness as those who deliver them. "Too many laymen speak about the preaching event as if it were a one-way street, as if the responsibility for what transpires when the Bible is proclaimed rests solely on the shoulders of the preacher. But that's not so! Effective communication demands competence from all parties."[6]

Adams is right about communication—the very definition of the word necessitates the reception as well as the trans-
mission of ideas. So even if the finest orator in the world would
deliver his clearest speech while facing only a brick wall, communication would not be taking place. No doubt many Bible
teachers would say they often feel as if they are talking to a
brick wall when they face their congregations, and many times
they would be right, because the people have put very little
preparation or effort into their end of the communication
process. Again Charles Spurgeon's comments are appropriate:

> We are told men ought not to preach without preparation.
> Granted, but we add, men ought not to *hear* without prepa-
> ration. Which, do you think, needs the most preparation,
> the sower or the ground? I would have the sower come with
> clean hands, but I would have the ground well-plowed and
> harrowed, well-turned over, and the clods broken before
> the seed comes in. It seems to me that there is more prepa-
> ration needed by the ground than by the sower, more by
> the hearer than by the preacher.[7]

Hearing the Word of God properly is a scriptural responsibility that many Christians do not realize they have
(cf. Matt. 13:9 and similar passages; Mark 4:24; Luke 8:18;
10:16; Rev. 2–3). And many of us who recognize that responsibility are unsure how to fulfill it properly. Below are
ten suggestions to help us become better listeners and
learners during the teaching of God's Word (most of which
are discussed more extensively in Jay Adams's book mentioned above):

1. "Test yourselves to see if you are in the faith"
   (2 Cor. 13:5). Only those who have been saved

from sin by grace through faith in Christ can truly understand the truth of God's Word (1 Cor. 2:14).

2. Confess and forsake your sin continually (1 John 1:9), because 1 Peter 2:1–2 says that we must be putting aside "all malice and all guile and hypocrisy and envy and all slander" so that we may, "like newborn babes, long for the pure milk of the word."

3. Prepare yourself for the message the night before by praying and getting to bed on time, and also by rising early enough to have plenty of time to get ready in the morning.

4. Through prayer and disciplined thought, adjust your attitude prior to the service so that you expect to hear exciting and life-changing truths from God (Ps. 119:18, 40, 96, 125, 162).

5. Eliminate any potential distractions that might hinder your attentiveness during the message (Rom. 13:14).

6. Make a concerted effort during the service to understand and retain as much as you can from the teaching, perhaps by taking notes and writing down in your own words the primary lessons you learn and the questions raised in your mind (cf. Ps. 119:11; James 1:25).

7. Practice and develop your skills of discernment by examining the teaching carefully, but remember to maintain a humble, teachable spirit (Acts 17:11; 1 Thess. 5:21–22).

8. Discuss the message with other Christians after the service, asking them questions and sharing the encouragement and challenges you received (cf. Rom. 15:14; Heb. 10:24).

9. Study the passage or topic further by discussing it with the teacher or other knowledgeable Christians, and by referring to commentaries and other helpful books.

10. Purpose in your heart to make any changes necessary as a result of what you have learned, pray about those changes, and practice them daily (James 1:22–25).

Praying with and for the Body

Corporate prayer was an important element in Old Testament worship gatherings (cf. 1 Kings 18:36; 2 Chron. 7:15; Isa. 56:7), and the early church continued that tradition. We find them praying together in Acts 1:14; 2:1, 46; 4:24, 32; 5:12; 6:4, and so on. The unity and power present in the early church was evidenced by its emphasis on corporate prayer, but it is also likely that such prayer was a *cause* of their great success. Some benefits exist when the church gathers to pray that do not when an individual prays alone, such as the proportional power of more voices raised to God and the instructional example of the public prayers of godly leaders (1 Tim. 2:8). The latter purpose is probably one of the reasons Jesus recited His lengthy High Priestly Prayer in the presence of His disciples (John 17).

All individual believers should be participating intently when someone is leading the congregation in prayer, rather than daydreaming or fixing their hair. But there are other ways in which we can contribute to the worship services through our prayers. We can pray before, during, and after the services that we and others would honor God and grow spiritually. We can also pray specifically for the preacher, like the man known as "Praying Hyde" did as a continual ministry early in this century. He met with missionaries and other Christian workers in India and prayed for extended periods of time prior to their speaking engagements. "Hyde knelt for hours in his room or was prostrate on the floor, or he sat in on a message and interceded for the speaker and the hearers."[8]

Some churches have groups of people who retire to a room during the sermon and pray for God to work through it. They then listen to the tape later for their own edification. These and other ways of emphasizing prayer in the worship service would cause the power of God to descend more fully upon our churches (cf. James 5:16–18).

Singing to Each Other and to the Lord

Ephesians 5:18–19 says we are to "be filled with the Spirit, speaking to one another in psalms and hymns and spiritual songs, singing and making melody with your heart to the Lord." And Colossians 3:16 says similarly, "Let the word of Christ richly dwell within you, with all wisdom teaching and admonishing one another with psalms and hymns and spiritual songs, singing with thankfulness in your hearts to God." Those passages both represent the twofold role music has always played in the corporate worship of God's people. It has provided challenges and encouragements to the members of the body, and it has provided praises and petitions to God.

The first role is largely overlooked, perhaps because it seems more natural to praise God through music than it does to speak to other people or allow ourselves to be challenged through it. But addressing other believers in music is biblical, according to the passages above, and God has often used the talents and passions of musicians to confront and comfort His people. The responsibility of each believer in this regard, therefore, is to think seriously about the lyrics of the songs he hears, to apply their message to his own life, and to be willing to use any artistic abilities of his own in the process of challenging others through music.

The second role that music plays in worship is to act as a special channel through which we can direct our tributes and requests to God. We are to "sing to the Lord," as it says thirty-three times in the book of Psalms. Revelation 14:3 and

15:3–4 depict the redeemed in heaven singing praises to God, indicating that all Christians will undoubtedly spend eternity doing the same. So why should we not practice diligently and repeatedly while we are on earth? We should, of course, and the corporate worship services are one place we can do that. When we have the opportunity, therefore, nothing less than energetic, sincere singing will honor the One whom we worship. And if we have instrumental or vocal abilities, we should be willing to place them at the disposal of the Lord for use in the church.

Observing the Ordinances of the Church

In the Old Testament, God gave the nation of Israel many rites, rituals, ordinances, or "sacraments" to observe as signs of belonging to Him. One such rite was circumcision, and the following passage shows how seriously God viewed this ordinance.

> God said further to Abraham, "Now as for you, you shall keep My covenant, you and your descendants after you throughout their generations. This is My covenant, which you shall keep, between Me and you and your descendants after you: every male among you shall be circumcised. And you shall be circumcised in the flesh of your foreskin; and it shall be the sign of the covenant between Me and you. . . . But an uncircumcised male who is not circumcised in the flesh of his foreskin, *that person shall be cut off from his people; he has broken My covenant.*" (Gen. 17:9–14, emphasis added)

When the old covenant was in force, no man could be a part of God's people if he did not partake in this ordinance of circumcision that God had established. The responsibility to participate in the other ordinances, such as the ordained feasts, was just as grave.

God has established two ordinances in the new covenant—baptism and the Lord's Supper—and He takes them just as seriously as the former rites. Yet, unfortunately, many professing Christians today think of them as merely nice suggestions that they can take or leave. On the contrary, they have been designed to be essential elements of the corporate worship of the church in which all the members must participate.

Baptism. The first way in which every believer must participate in the ordinance of baptism is to *be baptized* (cf. Matt. 28:19–20). This is simply not an option for anyone who claims to know Christ as Lord and Savior, contrary to the impression given by the masses of unbaptized church members and attenders in evangelical churches. When someone in the first century professed belief in Christ, he or she was immediately baptized (cf. Acts 2:41; 8:12, 36–38; 9:18; 10:47–48). As F. F. Bruce comments, "The idea of an unbaptized Christian is simply not entertained in the New Testament."[9]

That is why baptism and salvation are linked so closely together in some passages (e.g., Acts 2:38; 22:16)—not because the rite in itself saves anyone (it does not), but because it is the first step of obedience in which the believer outwardly identifies himself with Jesus Christ and His church. It is the initial sign of being a part of the new covenant. Furthermore, baptism is related to salvation in the sense that those who refuse it disobey a direct commandment of God and thus bring the validity of their faith into serious question (cf. John 14:15; 1 John 2:3; James 2:14–26).

So to say that every believer has the responsibility to be baptized is an understatement. But it is also important to note that our responsibilities regarding baptism do not end after we are baptized. We then have the responsibility to witness the baptism of others entering the body, confirm them in their outward identification with Christ and the church, and hold them accountable to the responsibilities they now have as members of the body.[10]

The Lord's Supper. This second ordinance of the new covenant is not linked in Scripture with salvation the way baptism is, but it is by no means less important. Whereas baptism is an outward sign of entrance into the covenant, the Lord's Supper (or Communion, as it is often called) is a memorial of the death of Jesus Christ, the event that initiated the new covenant and actually made it possible. And our Savior Himself commanded that we partake of the bread and wine that symbolize His body and blood. He said, "Do this in remembrance of Me" (1 Cor. 11:24).

Since that command came from the lips of Jesus Himself, it is not surprising that the book of Acts depicts the church celebrating the Lord's Supper repeatedly. In fact, Acts 2:42 says "they were *continually* devoting themselves . . . to the breaking of bread." The importance of this ordinance is further emphasized by Paul in 1 Corinthians 11:26–30.

> As often as you eat this bread and drink the cup, you proclaim the Lord's death until He comes. Therefore whoever eats the bread or drinks the cup of the Lord in an unworthy manner, shall be guilty of the body and the blood of the Lord. But let a man examine himself, and so let him eat of the bread and drink of the cup. For he who eats and drinks, eats and drinks judgment to himself, if he does not judge the body rightly. For this reason many among you are weak and sick, and a number sleep [in other words, they have died].

That passage makes clear that we must take Communion very seriously and approach it with the right attitude.

When we do, not only will we avoid the judgment of God, but we will also experience the special blessing this celebration can bring. Charles Spurgeon's advice is helpful: "Never mind that bread and wine, unless you can use them as folks often use their spectacles. What do they use them for? To look at? No, to look *through* them. So, use the bread and wine as a pair of spectacles. Look through them, and do not be satisfied until you can say, 'Yes, yes, I can see the Lamb of God, which taketh away the sin of the world.'"[11]

So the Lord's Supper is a blessed ordinance that every believer must partake of regularly to be a true worshiper of God. The words of songwriter Michael Card apply to all who desire to obey Christ in this matter.

> Come to the table He's prepared for you;
> The bread of forgiveness, the wine of release.
> Come to the table and sit down beside Him.
> The Savior wants you to join in the feast.[12]

Giving to the Lord and His Church

Giving of our financial resources to the Lord is both a solemn duty and a wonderful privilege. It is a duty because we have been commanded by God to do it (1 Cor. 16:2; 2 Cor. 9:7) and because He has warned that those who withhold gifts from him will face His severe chastening (Mal. 3:8–9; Luke 16:11). But it is also a wonderful privilege because God's pleasure and blessing rest upon those who give generously to Him (Mal. 3:10; Acts 20:35; 2 Cor. 9:6–8; Heb. 13:16).

According to the Word of God, the primary place that this activity should take place is the local church. Giving is very much an act of worship, and God has designed it to be an element of the corporate worship of the body. First Corinthians 16:1–3 says, "Now concerning the collection for the saints, as I directed the churches of Galatia, so do you also. On the first day of every week let each one of you put aside and save, as he may prosper, that no collections be made when I come."

The Greek term translated "save" is a participle from the verb *thesaurizo*, and our word "treasury" comes from the noun form of that word. It implies a central place where funds would be collected and kept. Therefore the King James Version translates this section of the verse, "Let every one of you lay by him in store." That seems to better capture the meaning of what Paul is saying: because if he meant that every one should put aside money on his own, he would have had no reason to tell them to do this "on the first day of the week"; nor would his reference to "no collections when I come" make any sense if they were individually retaining their money. How would Paul ever get the money if they had never collected it? Further, Paul's words in verse 3 indicate that some believers were approved by the church to handle funds.

So it seems clear that Paul was offering the Corinthians (and all Christians following) divine instructions regarding giving in the local church. As in Old Testament corporate worship (Ps. 96:8; Mal. 3:10), the offerings of Christians should be brought to the assembly so that the godly leaders there could apportion them for the work of the ministry. First Corinthians 16:1–2 and other New Testament passages also reveal some additional principles that should govern our giving:

Giving should be regular. Paul told the Corinthians that they should give "on the first day of every week." No doubt he knew that to make giving a regular occurrence would help us to be more consistently focused on God, particularly in regard to this important area of our finances.

Giving should be individual. By saying "each one of you," Paul emphasizes that giving is the responsibility of every Christian who has anything to give. This applies even to the housewives and children who may only receive a very small amount of income infrequently. Remember that the widow in Mark 12:41–44 gave only the equivalent of one-fourth of a cent, but she honored the Lord with her gift.

Giving should be planned. We are to "put aside" the money we will give to God, which is a deliberate, carefully considered procedure. Second Corinthians 9:7 says each one should give "as he has purposed in his heart," and the Greek word for "purpose" (*proaireo*) means "to set aside beforehand." As Jesus said when discussing money, "He who is faithful in a very little thing is faithful also in much; and he who is unrighteous in a very little thing is unrighteous also in much. If therefore you have not been faithful in the use of unrighteous mammon, who will entrust the true riches to you?" (Luke 16:10–11).

Giving should be proportional. Paul told each Corinthian to give "as he may prosper." Our giving should be proportionate to the financial blessings God has given us. For this reason, it is helpful to decide upon a percentage of our gross income as a regular minimum gift to the local church.

Giving should be sacrificial. That proportional amount we give regularly to the church should be one that strains our budgets enough that it can never be merely a token offering to God. And we must be willing to meet other needs that arise in the fellowship with gifts above and beyond that regular giving. To put it plainly, giving is only pleasing to

God *when it costs us something.* That is why the widow with her meager gift was so much more honoring to God than were the rich people with their lavish ones (Mark 12:41–44). Consider the description of the Macedonians' giving in 2 Corinthians 8:1–4.

> Now, brethren, we wish to make known to you the grace of God which has been given in the churches of Macedonia, that in a great ordeal of affliction their abundance of joy and their deep poverty overflowed in the wealth of their liberality. For I testify that according to their ability, and beyond their ability they gave of their own accord, begging us with much entreaty for the favor of participation in the support of the saints.

Giving should be cheerful. The last statement in that passage reveals the greatest reason why the giving of the Macedonians was so impressive to Paul and pleasing to God: they truly *wanted* to sacrifice for the Lord. Like worship in general, giving is only acceptable when it is done out of a heart of gratefulness and joy for the majesty of God and the goodness He has bestowed upon us. So Paul commands us in 2 Corinthians 9:7, "Let each one do just as he has purposed in his heart; not grudgingly or under compulsion; for God loves a cheerful giver."

Serving One Another in the Services

Although worship services are often not the ideal place to build intimate relationships with other members of the body (because of their size and nature), there are still ways in which we as individuals can serve one another in them. These primarily pertain to making the worship services more enjoyable and profitable for everyone there.

We can exercise the gift of "helps." First Corinthians 12:28 says that "helps" is a spiritual gift given to the members of the church, and that gift absolutely must be exercised in abundance for the worship services to run smoothly. Helpers are needed to prepare the Communion elements, aid baptismal subjects, monitor the sound system, maintain the buildings, watch the children, and assist with a multitude of other ministries. A worship gathering that honors God and brings people closer to Him depends upon *much* more than the preaching and music.

We can exercise the gift of "administrations." First Corinthians 12:28 also says that some members of the body are gifted in organizing and making practical decisions for the life of the church. We need people who can plan and decide upon various practical considerations such as the order of the service, the music, how the offerings will be collected and the visitors welcomed, etc. It is usually best for the pastor not to do these things, so that he may give himself to the Word and to prayer (Acts 6:1–6). It is important that the services be administrated properly so that "all things [may] be done properly and in an orderly manner" (1 Cor. 14:40).

We can show friendliness and hospitality to others. God wants the church services to be a place where people feel welcomed and loved, and the only way that will happen is if the individual members make an effort to be courteous toward one another and the visitors among them. Some of us can fill the roles of "ushers" or "hosts," ministering before and after the service to those who attend. Others can simply plan to talk to several others, including at least one person they do not know. We can extend an open worship guide or hymn book to a couple who came in late, move to free up seats for others, and show friendliness through a multitude of other small courtesies that make an important impact on the atmosphere of the service. Most of all, we must make sure to avoid the kind of critical favoritism described in this passage:

> My brethren, do not hold your faith in our glorious Lord Jesus Christ with an attitude of personal favoritism. For if a man comes into your assembly with a gold ring and dressed in fine clothes, and there also comes in a poor man in dirty clothes, and you pay special attention to the one who is wearing the fine clothes, and say, "You sit here in a good place," and you say to the poor man, "You stand over there, or sit down by my footstool," have you not made distinctions among yourselves, and become judges with evil motives? . . . If, however, you are fulfilling the royal law, according to the Scripture, "You shall love your neighbor as yourself," you are doing well. But if you show partiality, you are committing sin." (James 2:1–9)

There are probably many other ways in which we as believers can participate in public worship, but the ones described in this chapter are fundamentally necessary to any true worship. If we will pursue a biblical involvement in each one when we gather with other believers, we can avoid falling into the trap of pseudoworship described in this illustration by Don Whitney:

> One of the saddest experiences of my childhood happened on my tenth birthday. Invitations to the celebration were mailed days in advance to eight friends. It was going to be my best birthday ever. They all came to my house right after dark. My dad grilled hot dogs and hamburgers while my mother put the finishing touches on the birthday cake. After we had eaten all the icing and ice cream and most of the

cake, it was time for the presents. Honestly, I can't recall even one of the gifts today, but I do remember the great time I was having with the guys who gave them to me. Since I had no brothers, the best part of the whole event was just being with the other boys.

The climax of this grand celebration was a gift from me to them. Nothing was too good for my friends. Cost was immaterial. I was going to pay their way to the most exciting event in town—the high school basketball game. I can still see us spilling out of my parents' station wagon with laughter on that cool evening and running up to the gymnasium. Standing at the window, paying for nine 25-cent tickets and surrounded by my friends—it was one of those simple but golden moments in life. The picture in my mind was the perfect ending to a ten-year-old boy's perfect birthday. Four friends on one side and four friends on the other, I would sit in the middle while we munched popcorn, punched each other, and cheered our high school heroes. As we went inside, I remember feeling happier than Jimmy Stewart in the closing scene of *It's a Wonderful Life*.

Then the golden moment was shattered. Once in the gym, all my friends scattered and I never saw them again the rest of the night. There was no thanks for the fun, the food or the tickets. Not even a "Happy Birthday, but I'm going to sit with someone else." Without a word of gratitude or goodbye, they all left without looking back. So I spent the rest of my tenth birthday in the bleachers by myself, growing old alone. As I recall, it was a miserable ballgame.

I tell that story, not to gain sympathy for a painful childhood memory, but because it reminds me of the way we often treat God in worship. Though we come to an event where He is the Guest of Honor, it is possible to give Him a routine gift, sing a few customary songs to Him, and then totally neglect Him while we focus on others and enjoy the performance of those in front of us. Like my ten-year-old friends, we may leave without any twinge of conscience, without any awareness of our insensitivity, convinced we have fulfilled an obligation well.[13]

May we not be selfish children, but may we be loving, grateful ones who worship our Father in spirit and truth.

QUESTIONS FOR DISCUSSION AND APPLICATION

1. Review the section called "The Essence of Corporate Worship" (pages 121–25). How do you think an application of those principles could prevent a church from falling into "worship wars" over musical styles and other elements of the service?

2. How do you prepare ahead of time for Sunday worship? If you have not been doing so, how can you begin to?

3. Evaluate and discuss this statement: "The blessing received in a sermon depends more on the listener than the preacher."

4. Why is it true that for some people, 10 percent of their income is probably too small of an amount to give to the church?

7

USING OUR SPIRITUAL GIFTS

"What you don't know won't hurt you," the old saying says. That is true in some cases (especially during childhood). But according to the Word of God, it is not true when it comes to the subject of spiritual gifts. Paul told the Corinthian church, "Now concerning spiritual gifts, brethren, I do not want you to be unaware [or ignorant]" (1 Cor. 12:1). Through the Holy Spirit the apostle was telling those believers that what they didn't know about spiritual gifts *would* hurt them.

Ignorance about spiritual gifts in the life of any particular believer is harmful to the church as a whole and to that person. The church suffers because that believer has been gifted by God to play a unique role in the body, and the individual himself suffers because his usefulness and joy in Christ is dependent upon his exercise of that giftedness. On the other hand, if you as a Christian understand the truth in God's Word concerning spiritual gifts and practice it, you will make a significant contribution to the success of your congregation and experience increasing personal fulfillment in your walk with Christ.

Ephesians 4:7–16 is one of the New Testament passages that most clearly and thoroughly explains the nature and purpose of spiritual gifts. It says,

To each one of us grace was given according to the measure of Christ's gift. Therefore [the Scripture] says, "When He ascended on high, He led captive a host of captives, and He gave gifts to men. . . . And He gave some as apostles, and some as prophets, and some as evangelists, and some as pastors and teachers, for the equipping of the saints for the work of service, to the building up of the body of Christ; until we all attain to the unity of the faith, and of the knowledge of the Son of God, to a mature man, to the measure of the stature which belongs to the fulness of Christ.

As a result, we are no longer to be children, tossed here and there by waves, and carried about by every wind of doctrine, by the trickery of men, by craftiness in deceitful scheming; but speaking the truth in love, we are to grow up in all aspects into Him, who is the head, even Christ, from whom the whole body, being fitted and held together by that which every joint supplies, according to the proper working of each individual part, causes the growth of the body for the building up of itself in love.

That passage and other related ones in Scripture provide answers to a number of important questions about spiritual gifts. We will discuss each of those questions throughout this chapter, in the hope that you will not be unaware or ignorant regarding this essential issue.

WHAT ARE SPIRITUAL GIFTS?

Ephesians 4:7–8 says that believers have been given gifts by the Lord. The Greek word translated "gifts" (*domata*) is a common word that can have a broad range of meanings, but the context reveals that Paul is referring to *abilities that God has granted to Christians for the edification of others in the body and the evangelization of those outside the body.* A fuller picture of the nature of spiritual gifts is painted in 1 Corinthians 12:1–7, where Paul uses five different Greek words in reference to them. Studying those words briefly will help us to better understand what kinds of gifts believers have been given.

Pneumatikon (tr. "spiritual gifts," v. 1). This word comes from the Greek word *pneuma,* which means "spirit" and is often used to refer to the Holy Spirit. It tells us that spiritual gifts cannot be directly equated with the natural abilities we have possessed from birth. Rather, these spiritual abilities were given to us at our second birth, when we were born again by the Spirit of God. They may be in some way associated with our natural abilities, but not necessarily. For example, someone who has the ability to teach in a school setting may also be gifted in Bible teaching at the church, but another excellent educator may have little or no ability to exposit Scripture.

Charismaton (tr. "gifts," v. 4). This word comes from the word *charis,* meaning "grace." The point of the word in reference to spiritual gifts is that they come to us entirely through the undeserved favor of God and never as a reward for our sincerity or efforts at godliness (contrary to some of the teaching today about this issue). Paul emphasizes that truth in Ephesians 4:7 also when he says each one of us has been "given grace." Some have well defined the idea of grace with the three words "in spite of." God wants us to understand that we receive our spiritual abilities in spite of what we have done, not because of what we have done. An illustration of this is the Corinthian church itself, which had received an abundance of spiritual gifts (1 Cor. 1:7) despite its being filled with disharmony (chap. 3), sin (chap. 5), and false doctrine (chap. 15).

Diakonion (tr. "ministries," v. 5). This word denotes the idea of service and is also used in the New Testament to refer to those in the church who fulfill the role of "deacon" (an English transliteration of the Greek word). It tells us that spiritual gifts are given to us so that we might *serve* others. God has not given us spiritual gifts so that others might look at us and be impressed, so that we might feel better about ourselves, or even so that we might sit around and debate about them. They are not given to us for our benefit primarily, but for the benefit of others.

Energematon (tr. "effects," v. 6). Our English word "energy" comes from this Greek word, which emphasizes the fact that the power of God Himself is at work when spiritual gifts are exercised in the body. The effectiveness of our gifts is not something that we can ultimately control; we cannot turn it on and off as we will. God sovereignly dictates when His divine energy will do its work, and so we must be constantly dependent on Him for any good to come about when we serve one another.

Phanerosis (tr. "manifestation," v. 7). Finally, Paul refers to spiritual gifts as a "manifestation *of the Spirit*," meaning that they are given so that God's character and power might be revealed to the church and the world when gifts are used. We do not have spiritual gifts so that others will gaze in wide wonder at our prowess and ability, but that they would see the Holy Spirit at work in our midst and praise God for His grace and glory. As Paul said in 1 Corinthians 1:31, "Let him who boasts, boast in the Lord."

WHO GIVES SPIRITUAL GIFTS?

Paul uses those five words in 1 Corinthians 12:1–7 and the ideas communicated in their immediate context all emphasize

148

that *God the Father* has provided the body with gifts through *the Holy Spirit* as an exhibition of His sovereignty and grace. The apostle also makes this point repeatedly throughout the rest of the chapter (cf. vv. 11, 18, 24, and 28). And in Ephesians 4, he mentions three times that it is *Jesus Christ* who gives the gifts to the church, so all three members of the Trinity are involved in bestowing them upon us. This emphasis on the divine source of spiritual gifts is clearly intentional and is designed to promote unity in the body.

If you understand that any ability you have comes from a gracious God and that anything good you accomplish happens through His power alone, then you will less likely become arrogant as a result of your skills or successes. You will also be less condescending and critical toward others who have different gifts than your own, because you will remember that God Himself has organized the body according to His perfect plan, "just as He wills" (1 Cor. 12:11). If you are unhappy with some of the constituency of your local church and wish that they were more like you, then your problem is ultimately with God, who put them there and made them the way they are. Rather than complaining about their weaknesses, you should eagerly seek to use your gifts for their benefit and humbly receive the ministry God has designed for them to have in your life.

That is the point of the apostle Peter's exhortation in 1 Peter 4:10–11: "As each one has received a special gift, employ it in serving one another, as good stewards of the manifold grace of God. Whoever speaks, let him speak, as it were, the utterances of God; whoever serves, let him do so as by the strength which God supplies; so that in all things God may be glorified."

That passage tells us several times and in several different ways that God is the One who gives us spiritual gifts and enables us to use them. So when we do use them, we must do so as a humble recipient of His grace, recognizing that this "manifold grace" has provided the body with a large variety of abilities and personalities. Whether you speak or serve or fulfill any other ministry, you must give all the glory to God and be grateful for those who contribute to the church in other ways.

TO WHOM HAVE SPIRITUAL GIFTS BEEN GIVEN?

Ephesians 4:7 says that "*to each one of us* grace was given according to the measure of Christ's gift." All true believers have received spiritual gifts from the Lord. There is not one Christian in this world who does not have some ability to serve others in the body (cf. 1 Cor. 12:7, 11; 1 Peter 4:10). If you are a Christian—whether you are old or young, educated or uneducated, rich or poor, strong or weak, mature or immature—you have at least one spiritual gift (and you probably have more than one).[1]

Some believers don't think that they have any spiritual gifts, but the Word of God says that they do. Many believers don't know what their spiritual gifts are, but that does not change the fact that they have them. It is also true that we can neglect the gift that is in us, as Paul implies in 1 Timothy 4:14 (cf. 2 Tim. 1:6). But we all are gifted in some way, and we need to recognize this as the first step in using our gifts for the glory of God.

The fact that we all have been gifted by God means that each member of the body is *indispensable* in His kingdom plan. Paul makes this point further when he says that every believer receives spiritual abilities "according to the measure of Christ's gift." That phraseology helps us to understand some important truths about the use of spiritual gifts.

Every Gift Is Important

Anyone who sews or cooks understands the importance of measuring. A handmade dress produced by a seamstress who never measures the segments of cloth would end up looking pretty scary, and a cake made by someone who carelessly throws in indiscriminate amounts of random ingredients would only be eaten by the trash can. In order for a dress or cake to function as intended, careful measuring must take place.

Fortunately for us, the Scripture says that our Lord has wisely measured out the gifts He has given to the church. He knows just what He wants to produce in the church He is building, and He knows exactly what gifts are needed in the church to get the job done. He measures out the gifts He gives so that there will be no resource lacking in any particular body of believers. He has given you exactly the right kind and amount of giftedness so that you can honor Him and help your church to be everything it has been designed to be.

This means that every believer plays a very important role in the progress of a church. You will hurt yourself and the body of Christ as a whole if you do not faithfully exercise your giftedness. Just as one forgotten piece of cloth can destroy a dress and one missing ingredient can ruin a cake, so one ineffective Christian can keep a local church from functioning according to the biblical pattern.

Every Christian Is Unique

The idea that Christ "measures" the gifts in each church also indicates that we should not expect every believer to be equally proficient or successful in every area of service. There was only one man who ever walked the earth who had every spiritual gift in the greatest degree—Jesus Christ. John 3:34 says

151

that Christ received the Spirit "without measure." The rest of us, however, have received only a measure of giftedness that enables us to play a unique role in the body.

Not all Christians have the same giftedness. This is not to say that anyone should neglect the biblical responsibilities given to all believers by saying, "I'm just not gifted in that area." Every Christian is commanded to be involved in prayer, giving, loving confrontation, evangelism, and all the other duties that this book discusses. But we could say that while each one of us is commanded to be a general practitioner, each of us is also required to be a specialist in some area or areas. As you regularly and faithfully fulfill all the responsibilities of life in the Father's house, you should spend the most time and energy serving in those areas in which you have the greatest giftedness. And you should be very careful not to expect other believers to be as successful as you are in those ministries.

For example, some Christians are so gifted in evangelism that it seems to come naturally for them, and they regularly see people converted to Christ. But other believers find it very difficult to witness and hardly ever lead others to Christ. Both need to continue obeying the Lord by being involved in evangelism, but the one should not look down on the other because he does not evangelize as often or as well. Some believers also have a special gift of hospitality or friendliness so that they "have never met a stranger," as the saying goes. They make everyone who enters their presence feel loved and appreciated. Others, however, have to work hard just to avoid offending the people they meet. This may be because they have sinful patterns of thinking and action that God needs to change. But it may also be that despite loving others and wanting to develop friendships, something about their personalities or giftedness makes it a little harder for them. When you are tempted to judge others harshly because you see an area of weakness in their lives, remember that they may surpass you in other areas of giftedness and effectiveness.

Not all Christians with the same giftedness have the same amount of giftedness in that area. Among those gifted in evangelism, some will be more gifted than others. The same is true for hospitality and all other gifts. This may be especially important to remember when evaluating leaders and teachers in the church. Ephesians 4:11 says that God has given pastors and teachers to the church, and we should not expect them all to have the same abilities. Rather than comparing your pastor to others who seem more gifted, therefore, you should thank God for the abilities your pastor has and help him to make the most of them. The following words of Puritan commentator Paul Bayne concerning church leaders apply to any area of giftedness:

> The consideration of diversity of gifts does reprove those who will take mislike at this kind of gift or that kind of gift because it is not as they would have it. If one speaks calmly and stilly, though he lay down the truth soundly, if he apply not forcibly, they say "He is a nobody!" as if everyone should be an Elijah or a Son of Thunder. If others on some plain ground [they lack sophistication or panache] belabor the conscience, "Tush," they say, he is not for them, he does not go into the depth of his text—they could themselves at the first sight observe as much. As if every ship that sailed did draw a like depth of water. Yet all sorts of ships carry their passengers safe to their haven. So in pastors. Every one doth not have a like insight into doctrine. Yet all can be instruments of God to your salvation. This is an impudent, itching humor which, if you will be Christians indeed, you must lay aside.[2]

Recognizing that God has given differing gifts to each believer is important because it will help to keep you from both pride and despair. Be careful never to think you are better than another believer because you have a certain gift. And remember with gratefulness that your unique giftedness will always be indispensable in the work of the church. Also, if others are more gifted than you in a particular area, you should recognize that God has put them in the church for you to learn from them, rather than to be jealous and resentful at their success.

WHY ARE SPIRITUAL GIFTS GIVEN?

In Ephesians 4, after discussing the nature and recipients of spiritual gifts, Paul goes on to discuss their purpose in the church and the wonderful results that occur when they are utilized as they should be in a church body. Understanding this inspired instruction will help us to use our gifts biblically and will also motivate us to do so.

The Purpose of Using Our Gifts

In Ephesians 4:11–12 Paul says, "He gave some as apostles, and some as prophets, and some as evangelists, and some as pastors and teachers, for the equipping of the saints for the work of service, to the building up of the body of Christ."

Leaders are to use their gifts to equip the saints. Certain men in the early church were given special gifts by God, and they themselves became special gifts to the church as a whole because they trained the members of the church to do the work of the ministry. Their job was not to do the work of the ministry themselves, but to equip the saints to do it. The Greek verb translated "equip" (*katartizo*) can also be translated "mend" (Mark 1:19), "prepare" (Heb. 11:3), and "restore" (Gal. 6:1). It has the idea of filling in what is lacking, making something ready, or renewing something to usefulness. So the gifts that leaders have received should be used to teach, model, counsel, confront, and otherwise develop the serving abilities of the members of the church.

Members are to use their gifts to do the work of service. The difference between the leaders' role and the members' role in this passage is something that is often overlooked, to the detriment of the church. Many church members assume that they are paying their pastor to do all the evangelism, counseling, visiting, confronting, planning, and other ministries of the church. If someone has a need, they expect the pastor to meet it. If two people have a conflict, they expect the pastor to solve it. If someone needs to hear the Gospel, they expect the pastor to share it, and so on. But God has not designed the church to work that way. He has given pastors and other leaders the specialized role of preparing the saints so that most of those ministries will be carried out by the members themselves.

One church that understands this principle has a Sunday bulletin that reads like this:

Staff—[The names of the pastoral staff]
Ministers—Every Member

That approach to ministry in the church comes not only from Ephesians 4, but also from the biblical doctrine of the priesthood of the believer (1 Peter 2:5, 9; Rev. 1:6; 5:10). That doctrine means that each person in the church has the privilege of coming directly before God without a human mediator, but it also means that we each have the responsibility to fulfill the ministries that must go on in the church for it to be pleasing to the Lord. As a member of the body of Christ, *you* are a priest before God and *you* are to be a minister. The church leaders are there primarily to help you be effective in your service.

Throughout the New Testament, all believers are exhorted to serve one another in the many ways that contribute "to the building up of the body of Christ." We have already discussed in the previous chapter some ways that you can participate in service when the church comes together for worship, but God wants every Christians to do the work of the ministry every day of the week (Heb. 3:13). Husbands should constantly use their spiritual gifts to edify their wives and children in the home. Wives should use their gifts to build up their husbands and children. Children should find ways to encourage and serve their parents and one another.

If you have a home, you can show hospitality to your neighbors and other Christians. If you have a job, you can use the money you make to meet the needs of those who do not have as much. If you have a car, you can use it to bring people to church or other places they need to go. If you have a skill, you can make yourself available to tutor others who are weak in that area. Even if you enjoy talking on the telephone, that can be used not for gossip but to encourage and stimulate others to love and good deeds. Everyone in the body of Christ has spiritual gifts and various ways that we can use those gifts to contribute significantly to the work of the ministry.

Members are to use their gifts to do the work of evangelism. The building up of the body does not happen only by edification of other believers, but also by evangelizing those whom God is adding to the church by His grace. And that essential ministry of evangelism has always been done most effectively by the members of the church. To expect a pastor to do all of it is patently contrary to Scripture. Acts 2:47 says that in the early church "the Lord was adding to their number day by day those who were being saved." As the book of Acts unfolds, it becomes clear that people were being saved every day because the church members were witnessing constantly during the regular course of their lives (Acts 8:1–4; 11:19–21). Because this is is such an important task, upon which the health and future of the church depends, consider another lengthy but very helpful quote from Don Whitney:

> Why is evangelism expected of us? The Lord Jesus Christ Himself has commanded us to witness. Consider His authority in the following:
>
> "Therefore go and make disciples of all nations, baptizing them in the name of the Father and of the Son and of the Holy Spirit, and teaching them to obey everything I have commanded you. And surely I will be with you always, to the very end of the age" (Matthew 28:19–20).
>
> "He said to them, 'Go into all the world and preach the good news to all creation'" (Mark 16:15).
>
> "And repentance and forgiveness of sins will be preached in his name to all nations, beginning at Jerusalem" (Luke 24:47).
>
> "Again Jesus said, 'Peace be with you! As the Father has sent me, I am sending you'" (John 20:21).
>
> "But you will receive power when the Holy Spirit comes on you; and you will be by witnesses in Jerusalem, and in all Judea and Samaria, and to the ends of the earth" (Acts 1:8).
>
> These commands weren't given to the apostles only. For example, the apostles never came to *this* nation. For the command of Jesus to be fulfilled and for America to hear about Christ, the gospel had to come here by other

157

Christians. And the apostles will never come to your home, your neighborhood, or to the place where you work. For the Great Commission to be fulfilled there, for Christ to have a witness in that "remote part" of the earth, a Christian like you must discipline yourself to do it . . .

Think of our responsibility for personal evangelism from the perspective of 1 Peter 2:9: "But you are a chosen people, a royal priesthood, a holy nation, a people belonging to God." Many Christians who are familiar with this part of the verse don't have a clue how the rest of it goes. It goes on to say that these privileges are *yours*, Christian, "that you may declare the praises of him who called you out of darkness into his wonderful light." We normally think of this verse as establishing the doctrine of the priesthood of all believers. But it is equally appropriate to say that it also exhorts us to a kind of prophethood of all believers. God expects each one of us to "declare the praises" of Jesus Christ.[3]

So as a member of the church of Jesus Christ, you should always be asking yourself these two questions as you think about the purpose of spiritual gifts: How can I be served and challenged by the other members of the body (not just the leaders)? and Who in the church and outside of it can benefit from my abilities and resources?

The Results of Using Our Gifts

What happens when the members of a church ask themselves those questions and faithfully exercise their spiritual gifts in ministry? Ephesians 4:13–16 tells us of three positive results.

The church will become unified and loving. Paul says that spiritual gifts should operate "until we all attain to the unity of the faith" (v. 13). Many churches experience disunity and even "church splits" because spiritual gifts are not practiced in their midst in a biblical manner. People who are not involved in ministry find it easy to become critical of others, which leads to conflict and division. But when church members are serving each other through the power of the Spirit, a dependence upon one another and a gratefulness for one another develops and people are drawn closer together. (Chapter 9 in this book will discuss those ideas further.)

The church will become mature and wise. Spiritual gifts are also given so that the body might proceed "to a mature man, to the measure of the stature which belongs to the fulness of Christ. As a result, we are no longer to be children, tossed here and there by waves, and carried about by every wind of doctrine, by the trickery of men, by craftiness in deceitful scheming; but speaking the truth in love, we are to grow up in all aspects into Him" (vv. 13–15). Today Satan and his emissaries bombard churches with false doctrine and worldly philosophy, and unfortunately many churches seem to be like undiscerning, gullible children who adopt any new idea put before them. But in a church where there is an emphasis on understanding and practicing spiritual gifts and leaders who faithfully teach and train the members to do the work of service, a level of maturity can be reached that will create a formidable barrier to the Evil One and his schemes.

The church will become effective and successful. When we use our spiritual gifts, "Christ, from whom the whole body, being fitted and held together by that which every joint supplies, according to the proper working of each individual part, causes the growth of the body for the building up of itself in love" (vv. 15–16). When the members of the body fulfill the

159

unique roles of service for which God has gifted them, the church will grow. It will grow qualitatively in the effectiveness of its ministries, and in most cases it will also grow quantitatively by adding people who are being saved through hearing the Gospel or being served in some way by the body. On the other hand, the church is like a human body in that it cannot work effectively when its individual parts are not performing their function.

Are you doing your part in the building up of your local body, or are you squandering your spiritual giftedness and hindering the church from growing? If the latter, you need to realize that you are hurting yourself as well as the church, because you will receive the chastening of the Lord for disobeying His commands (Gal. 5:13; 1 Peter 4:10) and for not using the resources He has graciously given you (Matt. 25:14–30). Charles Spurgeon said, "I do believe it is before every Christian either to serve His God with all his heart, or to fall into sin. I believe we must either go forward, or we must fall. The rule is in Christian life, if we do not bring forth fruit unto the Lord our God, we shall lose even our leaves, and stand like a winter's tree, bare and withered."[4]

HOW CAN WE DISCOVER OUR SPIRITUAL GIFTS?

God commands us to make wise choices about the best way to use our time (Eph. 5:15–16), and so it is important to know where our giftedness lies so that we can focus on serving God and others in those areas. The following are some brief suggestions about how you can discern your gifts:

Study the Bible. Besides Ephesians 4, there are several other passages in the New Testament that discuss spiritual gifts in some depth (Rom. 12:3–8; 1 Cor. 12; 1 Peter 4:10–11). Read those passages and some good conservative commentaries on them.[5]

Pray. First John 5:14 says, "If we ask anything according to His will, He hears us." God has said that He does not want us to be ignorant regarding spiritual gifts (1 Cor. 12:1), so asking for wisdom in determining our giftedness is a request that is according to His revealed will.

Examine your motives. Jesus said, "If any man is willing to do His will, he shall know" (John 7:17). For you to have discernment regarding your spiritual gifts, you must seek that understanding with a humble heart that is open to whatever God wants you to do. If you want to discover that you have a certain gift so that you can be admired by people, or other selfish motives, then the process will be derailed from the beginning.

Evaluate your abilities. In the context of spiritual gifts, Romans 12:3 says that we should exercise sound judgment regarding the allotment of grace that has been given to each of us. A helpful way to do this is to take a piece of paper and make the following lists: Can Do (ways that you know you are able to serve), Have Done (ways that God has used you already in the body), Doing Better (areas of service in which you are improving), and Want to Do (ministries you would like to be involved in).

Ask others. The Scriptures repeatedly affirm the importance of receiving godly counsel (Prov. 11:14; 15:22), and the area of spiritual gifts is no exception to that principle. One of the most helpful things you can do to find out your giftedness

161

is to ask the opinion of several mature Christians who know you well and will give you objective, honest answers.

Take opportunities to serve. This suggestion is last on the list because you should only enter into a specialized area of service after you have followed the other suggestions. Certainly you should meet individual needs whenever they arise in the body, but don't dive into a ministry without an understanding of Scripture, prayer, the right motives, a careful evaluation of your abilities, and an affirmation from others that this is a ministry that matches your giftedness. If you do not see any "red flags" during those steps of preparation, then your experience serving in a particular area will reveal whether you have been gifted for it or not (cf. Prov. 18:16).

To close this chapter, consider this analogy: At a baseball game, the coaches and players do all the work in a combined effort to win, while the crowd looks on. Some onlookers are vocal supporters who say, "Let's go! You can do it! At-a-way!" Others are critics who say, "Can't you do anything right? I could play better than that." Still others are indifferent, like the wife who has been dragged to the ballpark by her husband and, looking up from her needlepoint, says, "What quarter is this?" These spectators contribute very little to the outcome of the game, though they may have strong opinions about how it should be played.

Unfortunately many churches are filled with people who approach church life as if they were at a ball game. They are content to let the leaders and some members do all the work while they themselves sit back and cheer, criticize, or simply pass the time. But God's Word makes it clear that life in the Father's house is not a spectator sport. We have been given spiritual gifts to *use* in service for others, and only by doing so will we work as a winning team. The Father has designed us all to be key players in His game plan for the body of Christ. So in that sense, every member should be a "full-time minister" in the work of the local church.

Questions for Discussion and Application

1. Why do you think God wants you to view your abilities and resources as gifts from Him? What difference will this make in your attitude toward them?

2. Think about other Christians who tend to "rub you the wrong way." Could it be that part of the problem is that you and they have differing gifts, and that you should learn to be thankful for the differences between you, because God has a purpose for them?

3. Have you ever slipped into the thinking that the leaders of the church are the ones who should do all the ministry, instead of equipping you and other members for the work of the ministry? What are some ways you can avoid that kind of attitude?

4. What do you think your spiritual gifts are? Make the lists suggested on page 161, and share them with one or more of your church leaders, so they can better equip you for the work of service.

8

CONFRONTING ONE ANOTHER IN LOVE

If God gave me the opportunity to exchange my life for the establishment of one truth among all Christians and I wanted to make my life count to the greatest possible extent, I would choose the truth of Matthew 18. . . . Here we have one of the most profound truths in all of Scripture. It happens to be the clearest step-by-step instruction that Christ gave to his disciples. If every Christian were committed to this principle, [we] would transform the church into a dynamic force in our nation and the world.[1]

The importance of loving confrontation as outlined in Matthew 18:15–17 for the life of the church cannot be overstated. The primary concerns that Jesus Christ has for His body are its *purity* (Eph. 5:25–27) and its *unity* (see next chapter), and neither of those can exist where the process in Matthew 18 is not practiced. That is because the obstacles to purity and unity are *sin* and *conflict*, and those maladies cannot be cured without the medicine of loving, biblical confrontation. If there is one thing we learn from the drastic measures taken by God to remedy sin (on the cross) and from the drastic measures enjoined on us by Christ (e.g., Matt. 5:29–30), it is that problems will never be solved by ignoring them. "Time heals all wounds" is one of the most inane statements ever made. Spiritual wounds may harden into scabs or scars over time, but their harmful consequences inevitably continue unless true healing occurs. Time by itself can never truly heal any wound of a spiritual nature, but the loving confrontation we will discuss in this chapter can and does perform healing when it is practiced in a biblical manner.

Through the years our pastoral and counseling experience has exposed us to hundreds of problems within local churches, and the solution to *most* of those problems has involved the application of one or more truths contained in Jesus' instruction to His disciples in Matthew 18:15–17. That passage says,

> If your brother sins, go and reprove him in private; if he listens to you, you have won your brother. But if he does not listen to you, take one or two more with you, so that by the mouth of two or three witnesses every fact may be confirmed. And if he refuses to listen to them, tell it to the church; and if he refuses to listen even to the church, let him be to you as a Gentile and a tax gatherer.

Our Lord tells us in that passage that the solution to sin and conflict in the body is confrontation that increases to whatever level is necessary to bring about change. Most people, including many Christians, shudder when they read about confrontation that may even involve a public rebuke of a sinning brother. The reason they find this repulsive is that it seems to them to be a very "unloving" thing to do. But on the contrary, the Scriptures teach that *confrontation is actually one of the fullest ways we can express our love for others.* Ignoring broken relationships or other sin in the body is usually the easier road for us, but it would be harmful to those involved and therefore selfish. If we genuinely care for others, however, we will be willing to sacrifice our own time, energy, and comfort in order to help them have a right relationship to Christ and others. Consider the following verses, which indicate this complementary relationship between love and confrontation by mentioning the two ideas interchangeably:

> Let the righteous smite me in *kindness* and *reprove* me; it is oil upon the head. (Ps. 141:5)

> Do not reprove a scoffer, lest he hate you. *Reprove* a wise man, and he will *love* you. (Prov. 9:8)

> Better is open *rebuke* than *love* that is concealed. Faithful are the wounds of a friend, but deceitful are the kisses of an enemy. (Prov. 27:5–6)

> My son, do not regard lightly the discipline of the Lord, nor faint when you are *reproved* by Him; for those whom the Lord *loves* He disciplines, and He scourges every son whom He receives. (Heb. 12:5–6)

Not only does confrontation benefit the one being confronted, but in many ways it also benefits the one who confronts. The primary way is the blessing and reward we receive when we please God by obeying His commands. And He has told us repeatedly in His Word to be involved in loving confrontation. In addition to Matthew 18:15–17, we are commanded to reprove or admonish others in some way in these New Testament passages: Romans 15:14; 1 Corinthians 5; Ephesians 4:29; 5:11; 6:4; Colossians 1:28; 1 Thessalonians

5:14; 2 Thessalonians 3:6–15; 1 Timothy 5:1–2, 20; 2 Timothy 2:14, 25; 4:2; Titus 3:10–11; Hebrews 3:13; James 5:19–20; and 2 John 9–11.

So loving confrontation is an essential element in the life of the church, and it should be "second nature" for each member to receive and give such admonition regularly. Because it is so important to the purity and unity of the body, however, Satan and the flesh work overtime to distort its practice, and many errors in the implementation of Matthew 18 have plagued the church since its inception. Because confrontation practiced in the wrong way actually exacerbates problems rather than solving them, we need to study Jesus' words carefully and understand exactly what He meant for us to do when sin or conflict arises in our midst.

YOU ARE YOUR BROTHER'S KEEPER

Jesus begins His teaching in Matthew 18:15 by saying, "If your brother sins,[2] go and reprove him in private; if he listens to you, you have won your brother." In that verse and throughout the rest of the passage, He uses first person singular pronouns to indicate that each member of the church is responsible to be involved in the resolution of sin and conflict in the body. Jesus says that if you know that another Christian has sinned, or if you have been sinned against by another Christian, then *you* need to confront that person about the problem. It is not right to turn a blind eye or a deaf ear to the situation, and it is not good enough to tell others and let them "handle it" for you. Each member of the body has a personal responsibility when he or she knows about a problem in the church, and that responsibility is to become a part of the solution. "Am I my brother's keeper?" is the question asked by the disobedient sinner like Cain (Gen. 4:9). God has always wanted each of us to be a "watchman" who warns our brothers of impending harm (Ezek. 3:16–21; cf. Prov. 24:11–12).

When we realize our responsibility to talk with others about their problems, however, many questions come to mind. Should I confront any Christian who sins or just those whom I know well? Should I confront every sin I know about, or just "the big ones"? What should be my attitude when I confront, and what method can prevent making the problem worse or making the person hate me? And because such negative outcomes are often possible, why should I even risk confronting someone? All those questions and more are answered by Jesus in Matthew 18:15. Carefully studying His words and other related passages will help us to become good "keepers" of our brothers and sisters in Christ. And because most problems in the body can be solved during this first step of "one-on-one" confrontation, we will discuss it more extensively than the other parts of the process.

Whom Should We Confront?

The kind of person Jesus says we should confront is a "brother." This term implies someone who professes to be a Christian and identifies himself or herself with the community of a biblical church (such as we described in chapter 3). It is a family term, of course, and so in its spiritual sense it refers to another member of our spiritual family. The local church is called a "household" or family in 1 Timothy 3:15, such terminology having been used for the covenant community of Israel (Matt. 5:47). And "brethren" is the term most commonly used in the epistles to refer to fellow Christians.

The apostle John uses the term "brother" many times in his letters, and the way he uses it helps us to understand its meaning in Matthew 18:15. He writes, "The one who says he is in the light and yet hates his brother is in darkness until now" (cf. 1 John 3:14–15; 4:20). First, his wording indicates that the term "brother" meant anyone who shared a common belief and fellowship with others in the churches. It was not limited to those who were close friends or compatriots. Even two people who did not get along were considered "brothers."

Second, John's words make clear that "brother" refers to *a professing Christian*, not necessarily a genuine believer. Someone who hates his brother is not truly saved, according to John, but that does not stop him from referring to such a person as "brother." This is important to note because we might have a tendency to judge that someone in the church is not a true Christian, stop considering him a "brother," and fail to follow Jesus' process in his case. But because true Christians do sin and because we cannot ultimately know the heart of another, we need to follow Jesus' steps of confrontation without drawing a conclusion about the spiritual state of the one who is sinning.[3]

Another passage that sheds light on whom we should confront is 1 Corinthians 5:9–11. There Paul is telling the Corinthian church to carry out the final step of church discipline, which involves putting an incestuous man out of the fellowship of the church. He writes, "I wrote you in my letter not to associate with immoral people; I did not at all mean with the immoral people of this world, . . . for then you would have to go out of the world. But actually, I wrote to you not to associate with any so-called brother if he should be an immoral person."

Notice that Paul says the process of loving confrontation is not designed for "the immoral people of this world," but only for a "so-called brother" (lit. "one who is called a brother") who is immoral in some way. Thus our responsibility to confront specific sin is limited to those who claim to be

Christians and share fellowship with others in a Bible-believing church.[4] When it comes to unsaved people or those who call themselves "Christians" but adhere to a false doctrinal system, our responsibility is to evangelize them. We may discuss some specific sin with them, but it would primarily be for the purpose of helping them to see their sinfulness and need for a Savior (cf. Gal. 3:22–24).

What Sins Should We Confront?

Jesus says that we should confront our brother if he "sins," but what exactly does He mean by this? Should we confront everything we see in someone else that could possibly be wrong, or should we only confront some sins that are "big ones"? Because of the potential extremes in this matter, it will be helpful to provide a clear and complete answer to this question. The broader scope of Scripture indicates that we should confront our brother when he commits *any action that is forbidden in Scripture and cannot be overlooked*. Explaining each part of that answer will help us to understand it sufficiently.

Any sinful action, whether "big" or "small," should be confronted (if it cannot be overlooked—see later discussion). The Bible does not distinguish between "serious" sins, which are open to confrontation, and "minor" sins, which are not. The Greek word for "sins" in Matthew 18:15 (*hamartese*) is a general term used for any kind of sin, and New Testament examples of sins that were confronted in the early church contain a great variety. They include heinous crimes such as sexual immorality, idolatry, drunkenness (1 Cor. 5:11), and false teaching (Gal. 1:9; 2 John 9–11), as well as many "everyday" sins like covetousness, hurtful speech, cheating (1 Cor. 5:11), legalism (Gal. 2:11–14), divisiveness (Titus 3:9–11), personal conflict (Phil. 4:2), deceit (Acts 5:1–6), and even laziness (2 Thess. 3:6–13).

Only sins of *action* should be confronted, however, because evaluating an attitude alone is extremely difficult with our human limitations and judging what is in someone's heart is simply wrong (Rom. 14:4; 1 Cor. 4:5), unless his words or actions clearly reveal a problem in his heart. Even in that case, it is still so hard to know exactly what is going on in another's heart that we need to proceed on the clearer basis of his action. Also, a statement like "you have a bad attitude" is frustratingly vague and does not provide a solid foundation for discussion of the problem.

We should confront someone only when he or she acts in a way *forbidden in Scripture*. That means being careful not to confront another based on a mere preference outside of Scripture (1 Cor. 4:6) or even a principle inferred from Scripture by "exegetical gymnastics" and wrongly elevated to a universal standard (cf. Rom. 14:1–12). An example of the latter would include the use of Deuteronomy 22:5 to say that women should never wear pants; that verse only forbids transvestitism. Another example is the oft-quoted but antiquated and incorrect translation of 1 Thessalonians 5:22: "Abstain from all appearance of evil." That verse speaks about avoiding false teaching, but Christians have often used it—for lack of actual biblical testimony—to condemn practices they simply don't like. The Scriptures speak to many issues clearly, and those explicit principles are a sufficient basis for reproof and correction (2 Tim. 3:16). In matters outside the clear teaching of Scripture, each person should be "fully convinced in his own mind" (Rom. 14:5) but should also be very careful not to judge his brother (Rom. 14:4, 10, 13).[5]

Finally, it is only necessary to confront sins that *cannot be overlooked*. Proverbs 19:11 says, "A man's discretion makes him slow to anger, and it is his glory to overlook a transgression." And 1 Peter 4:8 tells us that "love covers a multitude of sins."[6] If we took the time to confront every possible sin that other Christians commit, we would probably have little time for anything else. Inconsiderate words and actions, selfish oversights, and prideful thoughts expressed in some way are rampant in any body of believers and particularly common in family relationships. Many of those offenses do not need to be discussed, but can be overlooked. So how can we know whether to cover or confront in a particular situation?

Growing in biblical love and humility will help you to cover more and more offenses (especially those committed against you), and growing in biblical wisdom can help you to decide what sins should *not* be overlooked because of their harmful consequences. Love covers a multitude of sins, but sometimes sin throws the covers off. So we would suggest that when the following conditions exist, it becomes unloving and wrong to ignore the problem:

- If the sin creates an unreconciled relationship between you and the offender, so that you think often about the sin and think badly of him, then confrontation is necessary for the sake of unity in the body (cf. Matt. 5:23–24; Phil. 2:1–4).
- If you are not confident that the person is growing in the direction of Christlikeness by regularly confessing his sin and working to change, then confronting his sin may be the only way to expose his spiritual inertia and help him to avoid God's chastening (cf. Heb. 3:12–14; James 5:19–20; 2 Peter 1:5–10).
- If you know that there will be consequences of this sin that will hurt others in the offender's life, then for their sake you should make sure that he has recognized his wrong and repented from it (cf. Matt. 18:6; 1 Cor. 5:6–7; 12:26).

On the other hand, if you don't find the offense coming between you and the offender, if you know that he is confessing his sins and growing in the Lord, and you don't know of any harm that will come to others from the sin, then you should be able to cover it. (Of course, you may need to reevaluate the situation if it later becomes a bigger problem.) A question you could ask yourself when you think about confronting someone is this: In light of the next step in Matthew 18:16, would one or two more people of sound judgment consider this issue significant enough to go along with me? If not, then perhaps the problem should be overlooked at this time.

If you seriously question whether to confront someone or not, perhaps it would be better to be safe than sorry, and you should lovingly talk to the person about the issue. But as we grow in our love and humility toward others in the body, we should increasingly "learn to overlook a multitude of offenses, . . . recognizing that we are all sinners and that we must gratefully thank others for covering our sins as well."[7]

How Should We Confront?

When we know that God wants us to talk to another believer about a problem, it is then essential to approach that confrontation in a scriptural manner. If we do not, we will run the risk of complicating and intensifying the problem rather than solving it. Fortunately, God has provided for us a wealth of instruction in His Word regarding this issue. The following are ten words that represent biblical principles about confrontation and describe how we can do it in a loving manner. The first four are found in Matthew 18:15, and the rest come from other passages of Scripture:

Quickly. Jesus says, "If your brother sins, go and reprove him." He does not indicate that there should be any gap in

time between the knowledge of a brother's sin and the ensu-
ing confrontation. In fact, the tense of the Greek verbs implies the opposite—"go" is a present imperative that could be
translated "be going." Another passage in which Jesus emphasizes the immediacy of confrontation is Matthew 5:23–24: "If
therefore you are presenting your offering at the altar, and
there remember that your brother has something against you,
leave your offering there before the altar, and go your way;
first be reconciled to your brother, and then come and present your offering."

Our Lord followed that command with another that says,
"Make friends *quickly* with your opponent at law while you
are with him on the way." His way of dealing with problems
is not to postpone confrontation or other efforts at reconciliation, but to undertake them right away. While a problem is
ignored, sin and guilt can snowball until they become an avalanche destroying the sinner himself and others hurt by his
sin. The resolution God longs for will not happen until we go,
so we must go quickly.

There is one important step that Scripture places before
confrontation, however, and that is the step of self-examina-
tion. Jesus taught that you must be careful to not try to cast
a speck out of someone else's eye when you have a log in your
own eye. He said, "First take the log out of your own eye, and
then you will see clearly to take the speck out of your brother's
eye" (Matt. 7:5). So before we go, or even as we are going, we
must examine ourselves and confess any sin that we find in
our hearts.

Purposefully. By telling us to "go" when we know that a
brother has sinned, Jesus was saying that we should deliber-
ately go to him with the intention of talking to him about the
problem. He does not want you to meet with the person for

another purpose and broach the subject only if it comes up. Nor does He want you merely to "pray for an opportunity" to talk to him. Rather you should set up a time to talk to the person as soon as possible, and even tell him your goals for the conversation. This will eliminate any sense of deception that could arise from a less direct approach.

Verbally. The Greek word translated "reprove" in Matthew 18:15 is *elegxon*, which speaks of convincing somebody of something through words. The idea of the term is communicated well in the King James Version, which says "go and tell him his fault." The problem cannot be solved by certain facial expressions, subtle gestures, ignoring the person, or other nonverbal communication. It must be discussed with well-chosen words. Therefore, the importance of Scripture cannot be overestimated in the process of confrontation; God's words are the best-chosen words in the universe, and only they truly have the power to rectify the problem (cf. Heb. 4:12). When you go to show people their sin, make sure that you show them from the Bible.

Privately. The final principle from Matthew 18:15 about how to confront someone is that you should do it "in private," or "between you and him alone," as the Greek text literally reads. If the suspected sin is not a matter of public knowledge, then it should be discussed among as few people as possible. In fact, initially the confrontation should be "one on one" without anyone else knowing about it. The wisdom in this command of Christ is evident: It may not be necessary for anyone else to know about the problem because the sinning brother may repent or it may prove to be merely a misunderstanding. Therefore, the reputation of the offender can be protected. Also, telling other people about the problem before going to the person involved is essentially gossip.

Proverbs 25:9–10 says, "Argue your case with your neighbor, and do not reveal the secret of another, lest he who hears it reproach you, and the evil report about you not pass away." God wants you to be involved in the restoration process if your brother turns from his sin (Gal. 6:1–2), but it would be very difficult for him to trust you fully if you have told others about his problem before talking to him. (It would certainly be legitimate, however, to seek counsel about the issue without mentioning his name or otherwise revealing his identity.)

Reluctantly. Confrontation should not be something we are excited about or eager to do. "He who loves a quarrel loves sin" (Prov. 17:19 NIV); "It is to a man's honor to avoid strife, but every fool is quick to quarrel" (Prov. 20:3 NIV). Our attitude should be like that of the apostle Paul when he had to write a strong, confrontational letter to the Corinthians. Second Corinthians 2:4 describes that attitude: "Out of much affliction and anguish of heart I wrote to you with many tears."

Following the example of Paul, it would be good for you to express your reluctance to anyone you need to confront. You could say to him or her, "I want you to know that this is not something I enjoy doing at all. In fact, I would rather be at the dentist than discussing this problem with you! But I must do it in order to obey Christ and to show true love for you." When that kind of attitude is expressed, it makes it much harder for the other person to assume wrong motives on your part or to be angry with you.

Compassionately. Paul continued describing his attitude toward the Corinthians by saying that he had written his confrontational letter "not that you should be made sorrowful, but that you might know the love which I have especially for you." He wanted them to understand that his purpose in confronting was not to hurt them in any way, but to help them grow in the Lord and receive His blessing in their lives. He pointedly affirmed his love for those he reproved, and we should too. Proverbs 27:6 says, "Faithful are the wounds of a *friend*." Others will be able to accept your correction and instruction more easily if they know that you care for them.

Gently. Galatians 6:1 helps us to further understand how we should confront. "Brethren, even if a man is caught in any trespass, you who are spiritual, restore such a one in a spirit of gentleness." We must recognize that a Christian caught in sin is in a very precarious position and could be further "broken" by the wrong approach on our part (cf. Isa. 42:3). A lack of gentleness could tempt him to respond badly and cut himself off from the help he needs, but the presence of gentleness can work wonders. Consider these verses:

> A gentle answer turns away wrath, but a harsh word stirs up anger. (Prov. 15:1)

> Pleasant words promote instruction. (Prov. 16:2 NIV)

> Through patience a ruler can be persuaded, and a gentle tongue can break a bone. (Prov. 25:15 NIV)

Gentleness that makes the confrontation easier to take can be exhibited in a number of practical ways. You should confess any sin you may have committed against those you confront and ask for their forgiveness. If you don't know of any sin that you have committed, you could still ask them if they believe you have done anything wrong. You should make sure that your manner of speaking and the tone of your voice are calm and kind, rather than angry or brusque. You can explain how you have struggled with the same sin or others in your life, and even how someone helped you through loving confrontation. And you should compliment them on the good things in their lives as well as confronting them about the problems.[8]

Humbly. After Paul tells the Galatians that they should restore others in a spirit of gentleness, he adds, "looking to yourselves, lest you too be tempted." The Lord wants you to understand that you are just as capable of falling into sin as anyone else (even the same sin), so that you will enter into confrontation with an attitude of humility. In fact, you need to realize that you may even be tempted to sin during the confrontation! You could approach the situation in a wrong way and hurt the person more, or you could become prideful and look down on him without trying to see the problem from his perspective.

Proverbs 18:2 says, "A fool does not delight in understanding, but only in revealing his own mind." Sometimes we can be so intent on making our point that we continue making it even when some data surfaces and proves it wrong. That is why we should begin any confrontation asking questions rather than spouting platitudes. We must give others the benefit of the doubt and try to put ourselves in their shoes, just as we would want them to do to us if the roles were reversed (Luke 6:31).

Carefully. Confrontation necessarily involves words, and words can either heal or hurt. And as the old saying goes, you can't take them back. So in the potential "powder keg" of confrontation, our words must be chosen very carefully. The Book of Wisdom makes this point repeatedly.

When there are many words, transgression is unavoidable, but he who restrains his lips is wise. (Prov. 10:19)

With his mouth the godless man destroys his neighbor, but through knowledge the righteous will be delivered. (Prov. 11:9)

There is one who speaks rashly like the thrusts of a sword, but the tongue of the wise brings healing. (Prov. 12:18)

The teaching of the wise is a fountain of life, to turn aside from the snares of death. (Prov. 13:14)

Like apples of gold in settings of silver is a word spoken in right circumstances. (Prov. 25:11)

Do you see a man who is hasty in his words? There is more hope for a fool than for him. (Prov. 29:20)

Choosing your words carefully will involve studious prayer, thought, and planning prior to the discussion. If you stumble into the confrontation unprepared, you will undoubtedly end up hurting more than helping.

Prayerfully. Finally, as just mentioned, loving confrontation must be bathed in prayer, because God must work in the situation for it to glorify Him. Praying without doing anything is wrong, as we said, but doing anything without praying is equally wrong. Paul prayed for the churches before he instructed them regarding their problems (e.g., Phil. 1:9–11;

Col. 1:9–12), and Jesus prayed for Peter before confronting the disciple about his impending denial (Luke 22:31–34).

Why Should We Confront?

Jesus knew that the disciples' sinful flesh would make it difficult for them to obey His command to confront one another. So He reminded them of the benefits of loving confrontation at the end of Matthew 18:15. He said, "If he listens to you [recognizes his wrong and asks for forgiveness], you have won your brother." The goal of biblical confrontation is always restoration, and often the offender is won back to a life of holiness (cf. Heb. 12:10) and a reconciled relationship with others. In fact, sometimes a special bond of intimacy between two brothers develops because of a confrontation between them (Prov. 9:8), such as occurred with Paul and Peter (cf. Gal. 2:11–14 and 2 Peter 3:15). Moreover, a professing believer may be won to true salvation through a godly confrontation (cf. James 5:20).

Such are the benefits of loving confrontation, in many cases. It will not always work out so well, of course, and we will go on to discuss what we should do when it does not. But most conflicts and problems within the church can indeed be solved "one on one" when each believer is committed to dealing with them biblically rather than ignoring them.

BRING IN THE TROOPS

"If he does not listen to you," Jesus says, "take one or two more with you." If the "one-on-one" confrontation is not successful, then the situation has proved too difficult for two people to resolve alone. They need help, and "one or two more" believers are often able to provide sufficient assistance to settle the matter. But before we identify those people and the roles they play, it is important to understand exactly *when* they are needed.

Jesus describes the unacceptable response to rebuke by saying, "If he does not listen to you. . . ." "Listening" in this passage is a euphemism for a professed repentance, as evident from the parallel passage in Luke 17:3–4. The repentance mentioned there is only an apparent repentance exhibited by a willingness to admit wrong and ask forgiveness, because Jesus' teaching in verse 4 does not allow time for the offended person to "wait to see fruit" before forgiving. If the repentance should later prove insincere, however, then there would be cause for a further confrontation.

So the "one or two more" are only needed if the one being confronted does not agree that he has sinned or is not willing to change, and if the one confronting still believes the problem to be unresolved. If the offender acknowledges his wrong and asks for forgiveness, however, or if the confronter learns that it was a misunderstanding, there is no reason for another confrontation to take place. Both parties may want to seek counsel from others to complete the restoration, but such counsel would not be a part of the church-discipline process described in Matthew 18.

What Roles Do the "One or Two More" Play?

The text of Matthew 18 indicates that there are two purposes for involving additional people in confrontation. One is "so that by the mouth of two or three witnesses every fact may be confirmed" (v. 16). Since Jesus goes on to say that unrepentant sin should be made known "to the church" (v. 17), He wants to make clear that such a public exposure should not take place unless the fact of sin has been confirmed by more than one person. This is in keeping with the

Mosaic legislation in Deuteronomy 19:15, which Jesus quotes directly. The purpose of that law of witnesses was to eliminate the possibility of someone's being convicted on the basis of a false accusation from one individual.

For the confrontation process to proceed to the next level, therefore, the "one or two more" would need to be able to witness reliably to the fact that sin has indeed been committed. They could testify to the original sin that occasioned the confrontation (by discussing the issues or even playing "detective" in an attempt to settle the matter),[9] or they could testify to any sin that takes place in the confrontation. Though the original sin of the accused might be impossible to verify, he might exhibit ungodly words or actions during the course of the "investigation" and prove himself to be in need of church discipline.

Another purpose for the "one or two more," however, is revealed in the first words of Matthew 18:17: "And if he refuses to listen to *them....*" There they are pictured as attempting to admonish the sinning brother. When they know that sin has taken place in the situation, at any time during their involvement in it, their job is to lovingly confront whoever may be at fault (which in a dispute often includes both parties). As Jay Adams writes,

> The "witnesses" are not *merely* witnesses. They are first counselors who seek to reunite the two estranged parties. That is indicated in the words "if he refuses to listen to them." They are pictured as actively participating in the reconciliation process. It is when the refusal takes place, and only then, that they turn into witnesses. They do not appear as witnesses in this informal stage (to whom would they witness?); they will become witnesses if and when the matter is formally brought before the church. Paul makes

it clear that issues may not be entertained by the church unless witnesses are present (2 Corinthians 13:1).[10]

What Kind of People Should the "One or Two More" Be?

Jesus does not answer this question directly in Matthew 18, but scriptural wisdom tells us that the people involved in loving confrontation should be qualified, serious, and objective.

First, the "one or two more" should be *qualified* to counsel both parties and to participate in a restoration process if necessary. Galatians 6:1 says, "If a man is caught in any trespass, you who are spiritual, restore such a one in a spirit of gentleness." Spiritual people are those who have a working knowledge of the Scriptures (Col. 3:16; cf. Eph. 5:18) and who walk by the Spirit rather than the flesh (Gal. 5:16–18). So before you ask others to help in confronting someone, you should be confident that they will be able to provide some answers to the problem and that they are not harboring sin in their own lives (Matt. 7:4–5). They also must have enough personal integrity before others that they would be credible witnesses to the church if another step of confrontation becomes necessary. Obviously the leaders of your church should be qualified to be involved in this kind of discussion, but it might often be better to leave them out of the problem until it would become necessary to "tell it to the church." This would keep them from being overburdened with every problem in the local body and also would allow more members of the congregation to be involved in this important aspect of ministry.

Second, those who are asked to help in the process of loving confrontation must also be very *serious* about their involvement in it. Their attitude should be one that recognizes the special presence of Christ Himself in discussions concerning sin and conflict (Matt. 18:20). Also, the Old Testament law of witnesses states that when someone was convicted of a crime worthy of death, the witnesses themselves would be the first to bring down the heavy stones upon the head of the criminal (Deut. 17:5–7). This stipulation provided incentive for an honest, grave, and reluctant report from the witnesses—and the principle behind it should remind us of the seriousness of confrontation. The life of the accused is really at stake, even in our confrontations today, and so the "one or two more" must exhibit a sober attitude in their words and actions.

Finally, the counselors/witnesses should be as *objective* as possible. Because it is very possible that both parties are wrong in some way, and because people are tempted to respond wrongly when confronted, it would be ideal to take one or two Christians who are friends of the offender. If that is not possible, then you should at least try to take people who are not your own close friends, especially in a conflict. That way the one being confronted will not be tempted to think that you are "ganging up" on him by bringing only those who are on your side.

When we need help in confronting someone, it is important that we ask those who can make the best contribution to the situation. And if you should be asked to be a part of the "one or two more," then you must make sure that you are the kind of person whom God can use to remedy the problem.

THE LAST RESORT

Most problems in the church can be solved by the faithful application of the principles we have already discussed, but sometimes the leadership of the church and the body as a whole needs to become involved when all other efforts have failed. Jesus describes this role of the church in Matthew 18:17

when He says, "And if he refuses to listen to them [the "one or two more"], tell it to the church; and if he refuses to listen even to the church, let him be to you as a Gentile and a tax-gatherer." The fact that these steps are only a "last resort" can be seen in Jesus' terminology when He says, "If he *refuses* to listen to them. . . ." This is a different wording from the previous verse ("If he does not listen . . . "), and it indicates that the offender has shown a stubborn unwillingness to deal with the problem. It is only such a hardened refusal to listen that moves the process on to these latter steps. In fact, the words "If he refuses to listen *even* to the church . . ." later in the verse connote a sense of shock at the hardness of the offender's heart.

If this unfortunate refusal takes place in private confrontations, then Jesus commands us to "tell it to the church." Dropping the issue without doing that would be disobedience to Christ, because He wants the confrontation to increase in scope and intensity. And the involvement of the church body in this process includes an increased pressure toward repentance and a removal from the body if necessary.

Pressure from the Church Body

Jesus says that we should tell the problem to "the church," and that Greek term (*ekklesia*) is always used in reference to the whole body of believers. So it is clear that Jesus intends for the congregation to know about the sin. But principles from other Scriptures tell us that He would not want you to inform the church by interrupting the morning service with a spontaneous announcement or taking out an ad in the Sunday bulletin. Rather, you should discuss the problem with the leaders of your church and follow the procedure that they have developed to implement this command (cf. 1 Thess. 5:12–13; Heb. 13:17).[11]

The policy at our churches is that the elder board will first hear about the matter from the witnesses, give the offender an opportunity to answer the charges, and decide if it should be told to the congregation. If it is clearly an issue of unrepentant sin, then we will send a registered letter to the offender telling him about the process, begging him to repent, and warning him that his name will be mentioned to the congregation at a designated time. If he does not answer the letter or otherwise communicates that he is unwilling to work on the problem, then we will mention his name at the designated meeting or service, telling the members of the church that he has sinned and that they should pray for him, withhold fellowship from him, and call him to repentance.

This kind of public exposure and direction to the congregation is not only found in Matthew 18:17 but also taught and exemplified repeatedly in the New Testament (Rom. 16:17–18; 1 Cor. 5; Gal. 2:11–14; Phil. 4:2–3; 2 Thess. 3:6–15; 1 Tim. 1:20; 1 Tim. 5:19–20; 2 Tim. 4:9–15; Titus 3:10–11; 3 John 9–11). Therefore, every church should practice it out of obedience to the Word of God. But there are also many benefits of this wider confrontation that should motivate us to follow the Lord's teaching in this way.

First, telling the church is *good for those who sin.* Without the increased confrontation, they will probably not change and will continue to labor under the guilt of their sin and the chastening hand of God upon their lives. But this pressure from the church body is often used by the Lord to bring them to a joyous repentance and forgiveness (cf. Ps. 32:1–5; 2 Cor. 2:6–8). Also, because their previous network of accountability was apparently not sufficient to keep them from being trapped in sin, they will need specialized help and greater accountability if they repent and need to be restored. Widening the confrontation to the whole body allows the whole body to participate in such a restoration (cf. Gal. 6:1–2).

Second, this step of discipline is *good for the church*. When sin is confronted before the whole congregation, the whole congregation is challenged toward personal purity. Each member will be made aware of the gravity of sin (especially the seriousness of the particular sin that is being mentioned). Scripture commands, "Those who continue in sin, rebuke in the presence of all, so that the rest may be fearful of sinning" (1 Tim. 5:20). Also, the congregation will develop a respect for leaders who are willing to obey a difficult command from the Lord, and they will be instructed by example to obey the commands that are hard for them to obey. Paul told the Corinthian church that one reason he commanded them to practice church discipline on a particular person was "that I might put you to the test, whether you are obedient in all things" (2 Cor. 2:9).

That verse states clearly that whether a church practices public confrontation is an issue of obedience or disobedience to Christ. So if your church does not practice it, you have a responsibility to lovingly confront the leaders about loving confrontation! Show them this chapter or the verses mentioned in it, and ask them humbly to respond to you regarding this issue. They may be willing to listen, learn, and change their practices. If they are not, then that would be a reason to look for another place to worship. A church that neglects these commands of Christ is no better than a church that neglects preaching or the ordinances (cf. Rev. 2:14–16, 20–23). However, if the church you attend is unwilling to practice church discipline, but there is no better one in your area, then you should follow the process in Matthew 18 as far as you can personally and leave the rest in the Lord's hands.

Removal from the Church Body

When the church body does corporately confront a sinning brother and "he refuses to listen even to the church," Jesus says we should treat him "as a Gentile and a tax-gatherer."[12] Those were kinds of people with whom the Jews had no religious interaction. They were not considered to be a part of the covenant people of Israel because of their lack of commitment to God's law. So Jesus is basically saying to us that those who continue to sin after repeated confrontation should be put out of the fellowship of the church. They should be removed from membership with a public announcement and no longer allowed to participate in The Lord's Supper. The remaining members should be instructed to treat them as unbelievers by showing them Christ's love as they are able, but not having spiritual fellowship that would imply that they are right with God.[13] First Corinthians 5 contains an example of such "excommunication."

As with the other parts of the process of confrontation, this final step of church discipline seems to many to be harsh and unloving. People who hear about it are sometimes aghast at this procedure—one woman wrote a note to one of our churches saying "Jesus would never do that!" Of course our response to her was that Jesus Himself *told us to do it* in His Word. No godly pastor or elder ever enjoys the process of church discipline (quite the contrary), but we follow it out of obedience to Christ because we know that it is good for both the sinning brother and the church as a whole. In addition to the benefits mentioned above regarding public confrontation, putting someone out of the church is good for the sinner because God often uses this removal to severely chasten him and bring him back to the Lord. When he has been "delivered to Satan" (1 Cor. 5:5; 1 Tim. 1:20)—which means he has been sent out into the worldly realm where Satan rules (2 Cor. 4:4; Eph. 2:2)—it becomes much harder for him to maintain a semblance of moral purity or a false assurance of God's blessing. Being "out there," we hope, will help him realize his pathetic state and cause him to long for reconciliation with Christ. This is what Paul means when he says that as a result of "the destruction of his flesh, . . . his spirit may be saved in the day of the Lord Jesus" (1 Cor. 5:5).

The final step of discipline is also good for the church as a whole because people living in sin cannot help but have a negative effect on the spiritual health of the body. Paul also wrote to the Corinthians, "Do you not know that a little leaven leavens the whole lump of dough? Clean out the old leaven, that you may be a new lump" (1 Cor. 5:6–7). The purity of the church as a whole is dependent upon the purity of its individual members.

Jesus concludes His discussion of loving confrontation by emphasizing that when a biblical church enacts discipline in a biblical manner, it does so on behalf of God Himself and with His imprimatur. Matthew 18:18 says, "Truly I say to you, whatever you shall bind on earth shall have been bound in heaven; and whatever you loose on earth shall have been loosed in heaven." When our Lord's procedure is followed correctly, the decisions of the church correspond to the decisions of heaven itself (cf. 1 Cor. 5:4). Therefore, no one who has been placed under biblical discipline can legitimately walk away from that church saying, "God knows my heart, and He's on my side." Rather, the process of loving confrontation has shown him or her to be one to whom God is opposed (cf. James 4:6; 1 Peter 5:5).

Throughout this chapter, the importance of loving confrontation to the purity and unity of the church has been highlighted in various ways. That importance is well summarized in the following warning issued by John Calvin as he alludes to the whole process of confrontation in terms of church discipline:

> If no society or even a moderate family can be kept in a right state without discipline, much more necessary is it in the church whose state ought to be the best order possible. Hence as the saving doctrine of Christ is the life of the church so discipline is as it were its sinews; for to it is owing that the members of the body adhere together each in its own place. Wherefore all who either wish that discipline were abolished or who impede the restoration of it, whether they do this of design or thoughtlessness, certainly aim at the complete devastation of the church.[14]

Rather than tearing down our churches either by ignoring problems or by handling them in a worldly manner, may we build up our churches by confronting one another in love.

QUESTIONS FOR DISCUSSION AND APPLICATION

1. What are some reasons that it is loving to confront someone when they are wrong, or even if you think they might be wrong? Why is it unloving to not confront someone when you think they have sinned?

2. Have there been times in your life where you did not confront someone, and later you wished you would have? Have you ever confronted someone in the wrong way, and if so, what happened?

3. Matthew 18:20 ("Where two or three are gathered together in My name, there I am in their midst") is often quoted out of context to refer to prayer, but it is actually talking about the second step of loving confrontation

(which could also be called "biblical counseling"). Why do you think it is important to recognize the special presence of Christ when we get together to discuss problems, and how will that recognition help us to solve those problems?

4. Why do you think that 1 Corinthians 5 and 2 Thessalonians 3 say that during the third step of confrontation, the members of the church should withdraw themselves or withhold fellowship from the sinning person (see 2 Thess. 3:14 especially)? Is this a form of punishment, or a restorative measure?

PRESERVING UNITY
IN THE BODY

I urge Euodia and I urge Syntyche to live in harmony in the Lord. Indeed, true comrade, I ask you also to help these women who have shared my struggle in the cause of the gospel, together with Clement also, and the rest of my fellow workers, whose names are in the book of life. (Phil. 4:2–3)

In many ways, the church at Philippi was a model church. Concerning that group of believers, Paul wrote, "I thank my God in all my remembrance of you" (Phil. 1:3). That statement and others in the first chapter indicate that there was a special relationship between the apostle and the Philippian church. But as Paul's letter to them progresses, we begin to see some hints that the relationships among the church members themselves were not all that God wanted them to be.

For example, Paul exhorts them, "Only conduct yourselves in a manner worthy of the gospel of Christ; so that whether I come and see you or remain absent, I may hear of you that you are standing firm in one spirit, with one mind striving together for the faith of the gospel" (Phil. 1:27). He also writes, "Make my joy complete by being of the same mind, maintaining the same love, united in spirit, intent on one purpose" (Phil. 2:2). It becomes apparent in those passages that the Christians at Philippi were not as unified as they should have been; in fact, it seems likely that there was bitterness, resentment, and open conflict between some of them.

This suspicion is confirmed in Philippians 4:2–3, where Paul names two women who were involved in a conflict with each other. We do not know much about the conflict itself or its source, but we do know that it was serious enough for Paul to address it publicly. The problem between Euodia and Syntyche not only was hurting them, but was harmful to the whole church as well.

These two women have jokingly been referred to as "Odious" and "Soon-touchy," which implies that they were "problem people" likely involved in frequent conflicts. But notice that Paul describes them in Philippians 4:3 as those "who have shared my struggle in the cause of the gospel." The Greek word for "struggle" is an intensified form of the Greek word *athleo*, from which comes the English word "athlete." It speaks of a willing participation in an ardent competition. So Euodia and Syntyche had been earnestly contending for the faith in such a way that Paul considered them to be co-laborers with him. He also was confident that they were true Christians, which is more than could be said about some of the other church members to whom he wrote (cf. 2 Cor. 13:5). We know this because Paul referred to the two women as part of a group "whose names are in the book of life" (Phil. 4:3).

The point is that conflict and contention can occur between any two Christians, even if they have been committed to Christ and serving Him for many years. Also, disunity and dissension can happen in any church body, no matter how faithful that church has been to the Lord in the past. In fact, "church splits" sometimes begin with fights between those who formerly worked together in the body when it was growing and otherwise successful.

How does this happen? If we want to avoid such disunity in the church, it will be helpful for us to understand how the normal flow of human relationships can turn into a flood of seemingly irreparable discord. The answer is *a failure to resolve interpersonal conflicts biblically.* Some form of conflict is inevitable in any relationship involving two sinful people, but a proper approach to that difficulty will resolve it and bring the parties closer together. If an initial conflict is not handled properly, however, the problem will begin snowballing and eventually lead to an avalanche of disharmony.

If you were driving and a red light appeared on the dashboard, you could respond in several different ways. You could ignore the light and keep on driving, you could smash the light with a hammer, or you could find a mechanic to look at your car. If the problem was that your radiator was leaking, any solution other than taking the car to a mechanic would only intensify the problem. Continuing to drive the car would turn a minor problem into a major one.

That is what happens when Christians develop severe interpersonal conflicts and churches end up splitting. An initial conflict was not resolved biblically. The problem grew, was still not resolved properly, and so on.

A typical example is a wife who becomes distressed at something her husband does. Instead of informing him of her complaint in a loving fashion, she pushes it under the surface and pretends that it doesn't exist. In spite of all her efforts to ignore the problem, however, she still thinks about it. And her thinking about it affects the way she reacts and speaks and relates to her husband. Because her husband senses that something is wrong and because he doesn't like the way she is treating him, he asks her, "What's the problem?" When she answers, "Nothing," her refusal to talk about it frustrates him, and so he angrily demands that she do so, which irritates her even further, and so on. Soon the molehill has become a mountain and the small rift between them has become a chasm. The problem probably would have never progressed to this point, however, if she had properly addressed the initial trouble.

Another example of mishandling a problem, and actually intensifying it, is a person who is offended by something another church member has said. Instead of approaching the problem biblically, the offended person gets on the telephone and tells someone else how this certain individual has mistreated him. Back comes the reply, "Isn't that something? You know, he did the same thing to me." Soon these two gossips are calling two other people and spreading the news about the one who has offended them. The rumors spread, and the problem is only compounded.

What happened between Euodia and Syntyche was probably something similar. A small matter of dispute had developed into a big enough problem that news of it spread to Rome, where Paul wrote his letter to the Philippians. Because this conflict was a matter of public knowledge, Paul addressed it openly in his letter and suggested some divinely inspired solutions to the problem. Understanding his instruction to the church members at Philippi will help us to avoid and resolve conflicts in our churches today. God has given us this passage to assist us in "being diligent to preserve the unity of the Spirit in the bond of peace" (Eph. 4:3).

THE PRINCIPLE OF MUTUAL RESPONSIBILITY

Paul says, "I urge Euodia and I urge Syntyche to live in harmony." He considers them *both* responsible for the unreconciled situation between them, a fact that he emphasizes by repeating the verb "urge" with each of their names. In no way does Paul intimate that one person is all wrong and the other person is all right. He was very careful not to take sides, because he knew that both of them were to blame in some way for the problem. Euodia may have been the one who originally snubbed or criticized Syntyche. But if Syntyche had responded wrongly toward Euodia's sin, became resentful toward her, or gossiped about the problem, then Syntyche was sinning also.

If you do not respond to mistreatment and the resulting resentment in a biblical manner, then you are just as wrong as the one who is mistreating you. "It takes two to tango," the old saying goes, and we could also say, "It takes two to tangle." In most dances of disunity, both partners are out of step in some way. It will be helpful for us to consider some wrong responses to conflict that often compound a problem, so that we can identify them in ourselves and others and work on eliminating them.

The ways we often contribute to conflict can be grouped into the three categories of retaliation, inaction, and unwise confrontation.

Retaliation

When people have hurt us, our tendency is to strike back at them in some way. This tendency is a product of our sinful flesh (Gal. 5:19–20), which we must always fight through the power of the Spirit (Gal. 5:22–23). Paul summarized the teaching of Christ on this issue when he wrote to the Romans, "Bless those who persecute you; bless and curse not. . . . Never pay back evil for evil to anyone. . . . Never take your own revenge, beloved, but leave room for the wrath of God, for it is written, 'Vengeance is Mine, I will repay,' says the Lord. 'But if your enemy is hungry, feed him, and if he is thirsty, give him a drink'" (Rom. 12:14–20).

Those and other passages *command* us never to retaliate against someone who has hurt us. Retaliation is always a sin against the other person and against God. Yet we often add this sin to the initial sin and thereby make the problem much worse. This can be done through actions that range from punching the offender in the face to ignoring him, but it most often happens through our *words*. We often retaliate with our mouths by sending overt or subtle insults toward those who have offended us (cf. Prov. 9:7; James 3:8–10), or by speaking negatively of them to others who do not need to be involved in the situation (cf. Prov. 25:9; Matt. 18:15).

Inaction

Retaliation is not the only response that worsens conflict. You can restrain yourself from retaliating and still make a situation worse by doing nothing. This is a common pitfall among Christians. Trying hard to "turn the other cheek," they often ignore an offense because it would be time-consuming and difficult to confront it. Likewise, when they are the offender, they often ignore the problem, waiting instead for the other person to come to them or hoping that he will somehow forget about it. But the Scriptures say that when an unreconciled offense exists between you and another Christian, inaction is totally unacceptable. Whether you are the offender or the offended, the Bible says that you should never run away from the other person or a problem that harms your relationship, but you should go to the other party and do what you can to solve the problem.

Matthew 5:23–24 says, "If therefore you are presenting your offering at the altar, and there remember that your brother has something against you, leave your offering there before the altar, and *go* your way; first be reconciled to your brother, and then come and present your offering." And Matthew 18:15 says, "If your brother sins [against you], *go* and reprove him in private; if he listens to you, you have won your brother." When an offense occurs between two brothers in Christ that cannot be overlooked or "covered" in love, then the worst thing to do at that time is nothing.[1] Abstaining from retaliation is commendable, but it alone will not solve most problems in the body. Conflicts among members of the church must be confronted and discussed in love so that reconciliation can take place.

Unwise Confrontation

Sometimes believers recognize the sinfulness of revenge and the necessity of doing something about the problem, but then end up attacking it in the wrong way. The manner, content, or timing of their confrontation may not be entirely biblical, and this often exacerbates the conflict as much as retaliation or inaction would. The following story, adapted from one told by author and speaker Jay Adams, illustrates how this can happen:

John and Mary are a married couple having trouble getting along with each other. They are both Christians, but it is evident to both of them (and others) that a certain coolness has set in between them. As John is riding the train to work one morning, the Lord begins to work on his heart, and John starts to think about his marriage. He knows that something is wrong between him and Mary. For a long time he has tried to ignore the problem, but that has not solved it. So he decides that when he gets home that night, he is going to talk to her about it. He is determined to get it out in the open and solve their break in communication.

During that day, Mary also begins to do some thinking, and God convicts her about her attitude toward John. She comes to the conclusion that something has to be done between the two of them. Yes, she decides, she will try to talk to John that night when he gets home. Things are going to be different.

During that day, however, certain unplanned events take place—a series of minor catastrophes. She starts sweeping the rug, and the sweeper breaks down. Her three-year-old son decides to climb up the living room curtains and pulls the drapery rods out of the wall. She also receives several telephone calls that are disturbing and time-consuming. By two in the afternoon she still has not accomplished what she hoped to finish by ten in the morning. Then, to top it all off, the phone rings as she prepares supper, and while she is on the phone, one of her pots boils over!

When John walks through the door at 5:30, Mary is in the kitchen on her knees, trying to chip their baked-on supper off the stove. Intent on solving their marriage problems but paying little attention to her circumstance, John announces, "Mary, there's something wrong with our marriage." Mary responds at the top of her lungs, "You're right there's something wrong with our marriage! And if you ever come in here like that again, there won't be any marriage!" Stunned, John thinks, *So this is what I get for trying to improve our marriage!* Hurt, frustrated, and now seething with anger, he stalks into the living room, sits down, and sulks behind the protection of the daily newspaper.

While John sits there stewing, God is dealing with Mary's heart out in the kitchen. She knows that her response to John was contrary to God's Word. So she asks God for forgiveness and with a heavy heart walks into the living room to seek John's forgiveness. "John, remember what happened when you came home tonight?" To which he roars, "Yes, I remember what happened when I came home tonight, and if it ever happens again, I won't ever come home again!"

John and Mary have the right idea in determining to address the problems between them, but they confront one another in an unwise manner and therefore make the problem worse. Notice too how they *both* are responsible for the growing conflict. Resolving the conflict, therefore, requires starting with a mutual recognition of fault and confession. Until that happens, as in the case of Euodia and Syntyche in Philippians 4, the dissension between them will grow, and more and more people in the church will likely be pulled into the struggle.

If you find yourself involved in a conflict within the church, the first thing you should do is examine yourself to see what log might be in your own eye (Matt. 7:1–5). And if you have the opportunity to help others resolve a conflict, make sure that you start by helping both parties to see their responsibilities in the problem and its solution.

TWO PEOPLE WITH THE SAME MIND

Since conflicts are compounded by retaliation, inaction, and unwise confrontation, how can we change in the midst of those wrong responses and begin to solve the problem rather than make it worse? And more importantly, how can we prevent those wrong responses from happening in the first place?

The key to all godly conduct is the right kind of *thinking* (Rom. 12:2; Eph. 4:23), and realizing unity in the body is no exception. Paul instructs Euodia and Syntyche to "live in harmony in the Lord." The most literal translation of that command in the Greek text is "to think the same thing." The Lord tells us through this passage that the solution to disunity is for everyone in the body to be "of the same mind," as some other translations say. But how is this possible when everyone in the church is so different? Is Paul saying that we have to think exactly alike about every issue and every situation? Can we not have varying personalities and opinions?

The answer to those questions appears earlier in Philippians where Paul explains clearly what he means by "thinking the same thing." He uses that same Greek phrase in this command to the church:

> Make my joy complete by *being of the same mind*, maintaining the same love, united in spirit, intent on one purpose. Do nothing from selfishness or empty conceit, but with humility of mind let each of you regard one another as more important than himself; do not merely look out for your own personal interests, but also for the interests of others. Have this attitude in yourselves which was also in Christ Jesus. (Phil. 2:2–5)

The "same mind" that God wants us to have in the body is *the mind of Christ*, in which we regard others as more important than ourselves and seek to care for their needs more than our own. There should indeed be much variety in opinion, personality, and giftedness in the body of Christ, but even that diversity is intended by God to help us care for one another better (1 Cor. 12:14–27). If we all had the attitude of humility that was in Jesus Christ, then our differences would only be used to balance one another and help one another to grow, rather than to cause division. So to prevent and resolve conflict, we must work hard to cultivate the attitude of Christ. In the next three verses, Paul describes the humility of our Lord in more detail, so that we can understand His example and emulate it better: Jesus Christ, "although He existed in the form of God, did not regard equality with God a thing to be grasped, but emptied Himself, taking the form of a bond-servant, and being made in the likeness of men. And being found in appearance as a man, He humbled Himself by becoming obedient to death, even death on a cross" (Phil. 2:6–8).

Each of those verses describes the attitude of Christ related to His incarnation, when He walked the earth "leaving [us] an example [that we should] follow in His steps" (1 Peter 2:21). Philippians 2:6 describes His attitude in eternity past when He made the decision to become a man in the fullness of time according to the "eternal covenant" among the Trinity (Titus 1:1–2; Heb. 9:12–13; 13:20); verse 7 pictures that great transition in which He went from a throne in a holy heaven to a trough in a hate-filled world (Luke 2:10–12); and verse 8 tells us that when men failed to recognize who He was or treat Him as He deserved, He still surrendered Himself to an agonizing death on their behalf (Luke 23:33–34; 1 Peter 2:21–25).

The common factor throughout the earthly life of our Example was that He viewed the needs of others as more important than His own comfort or happiness. The mind of Christ was that of an unselfish servant intent on doing the will of God (Matt. 20:28; John 5:30). It was a mind filled with concern for other people. So to "be of the same mind in the Lord" means that both parties involved in a disagreement should focus their concern on the other person, rather than on themselves and their rights or desires. In Philippians 4:2, therefore, Paul is urging Euodia and Syntyche to stop being selfish in their thinking. He says, in effect, "Euodia, it's time for you to think about what you can do for Syntyche instead of what she can do for you. And Syntyche, you need to start considering what is best for Euodia."

Paul knew that God created our minds in such a way that we will always be thinking. Your mind is seldom, if ever, a vacuum. You are thinking either constructive thoughts or destructive thoughts. When you reflect on your day, you either think selfish thoughts, like how someone has mistreated you when you deserve better, or you think unselfish thoughts, like how you could serve the other person and meet his needs. Moreover, it is most often true that your feelings and actions toward another person will be in accord with the nature of your thoughts about him. If you consider him your servant and focus on what he should be doing for you, then your relationship with him will inevitably deteriorate as soon as he is not serving you the way you like. If you regard yourself as his servant, however, you will be able to help him in some way regardless of how he treats you, and your relationship will probably improve because he will appreciate your humility and learn from it himself (cf. Rom. 12:17–21).

Since having the mind of Christ toward others is essential for preserving the unity of the body, it will be helpful to briefly consider some practical ways that we can exhibit a servant's attitude in our thinking.

Hopefulness

Love "believes all things, hopes all things," according to 1 Corinthians 13:7. It is biblical to give others "the benefit of the doubt"—especially Christians who have the Holy Spirit working in them. Your attitude toward others in the church should be that they are innocent until proven guilty, and even then you should realize that your ability to judge is very limited because of your human finiteness and fallenness. Those limitations are what Paul had in mind when he wrote this condemnation of the sin of judging:

But to me it is a very small thing that I should be examined by you, or by any human court; in fact, I do not even examine myself. I am conscious of nothing against myself, yet I am not by this acquitted; but the one who examines me is the Lord. Therefore do not go on passing judgment before the time, but wait until the Lord comes who will both bring to light the things hidden in the darkness and disclose the motives of men's hearts; and then each man's praise will come to him from God. (1 Cor. 4:3–5)

It is not always wrong to make a judgment about someone else in your mind; in fact, sometimes it is necessary to do so, as we see in 1 Corinthians 5:12. But back in chapter 4, Paul tells us that there are some things that we are unable to judge and therefore should not try to judge. They are "the things hidden in the darkness" (that which has not been revealed in God's Word—see v. 5) and "the motives of men's hearts" (that which is known only to the other person and to God). Judgments based on such things are sinful and lead to division in the body (v. 6). And so God wants you to guard your mind against the common tendency to judge what is in someone's heart or to draw a negative conclusion about another too quickly, before you have all the facts. Realize that your sinful flesh makes you prone to think the best of yourself and the worst of everyone else, and seek to reverse that pattern through prayer and self-discipline.[2]

One way to do that is through the kind of loving confrontation discussed in chapter 8, because often the biblical replacement for sinful judging is talking with the other person openly about the problem. But an attitude of hopefulness will also enable you to overlook or cover many offenses (as we also discussed in chapter 8), because you will be confident that God is working in the lives of other Christians and be able to trust Him in various situations without having to resort to confrontation.

Graciousness

Even when offenses need to be confronted and conflicts resolved through discussion with one another, one who has the mind of Christ will always approach those situations wanting to treat others as he would like to be treated (Luke 6:31). You must also endeavor to relate to others with the grace that Christ has exhibited to you, as Paul says in Ephesians.

> Let all bitterness and wrath and anger and clamor and slander be put away from you, along with all malice. And be kind to one another, tender-hearted, forgiving each other, just as God in Christ also has forgiven you. Therefore be imitators of God, as beloved children; and walk in love, just as Christ also loved you, and gave Himself up for us, an offering and a sacrifice to God as a fragrant aroma. (Eph. 4:31–5:2)

Consider also a similar passage from the book of Colossians.

> And so, as those who have been chosen of God, holy and beloved, put on a heart of compassion, kindness, humility, gentleness and patience; bearing with one another, and forgiving each other, whoever has a complaint against any one; just as the Lord forgave you, so also should you. And beyond all these things put on love, which is the perfect bond of unity. And let the peace of Christ rule in your hearts, to which indeed you were called in one body; and be thankful. (Col. 3:12–15)[3]

Prayerfulness

No one can have the mind of Christ without being a prayerful person. When you praise God in prayer, you will find a gratefulness developing in your heart that will make it harder for you to be frustrated with others. When you constantly confess your own sins to God, you will not be as quick to be offended by the sins of others. When you intercede for the needs of other believers, you will be focused on them rather than yourself and will have the right attitude even if problems arise between you.

This unselfish mindset of a hopeful, gracious, and prayerful servant is not easy to generate or maintain. Paul knew that, and so in Philippians 4:2 he urges Euodia and Syntyche to "live in harmony *in the Lord*." Those two women could not possibly solve their problem through their own strength. Nor can we preserve the unity of the body in our own strength. Through prayerful dependence on God, we must realize that we can only overcome sin and walk in newness of life through the divine resources that we receive by His power and grace. We who are proud and selfish can become humble and unselfish. We who desire to be served can become servants. And interpersonal conflicts in the body can be solved, but only by the power of Jesus Christ working in us and enabling us to have His mind toward one another.

BLESSED ARE THE PEACEMAKERS

In Philippians 4:3, Paul indicates that some interpersonal problems may be solved only with the help of others. After addressing Euodia and Syntyche directly about their conflict, he then turns to other Christians in the Philippian congregation and says, "Indeed, true comrade, I ask you also to help these women, . . . together with Clement also, and the rest of my fellow workers."

Seek Help from Others

Apparently, Euodia and Syntyche had not sought help from anyone. Perhaps they thought no one knew about their problem or were too embarrassed to admit that they had a conflict they could not solve on their own. Maybe they were afraid that others would think less of them, gossip about them, or even reject them. Or they might have had the opinion that soliciting aid from others was unspiritual in some way. *After all*, they may have thought, *with the Lord's help we should be able to solve our own difficulties.* Whatever the reason, the words of Paul imply that the two women had not turned to their pastor or elders or other mature Christians for counsel and direction.

Their neglect of such help undoubtedly contributed to the growth of the problem between them, because the Scriptures say repeatedly that we need the aid and advice of others in our lives.

> Where there is no guidance, the people fall, but in abundance of counselors there is victory. (Prov. 11:14)

> The way of a fool is right in his own eyes, but a wise man is he who listens to counsel. (Prov. 12:15)

> Without consultation, plans are frustrated, but with many counselors they succeed. (Prov. 15:22)

> Listen to counsel and accept discipline, that you may be wise the rest of your days. (Prov. 19:20)

> If your brother sins [against you], go and reprove him in private. . . . But if he does not listen to you, take one or two more with you. (Matt. 18:15–16)

> And concerning you, my brethren, I myself also am convinced that you yourselves are full of goodness, filled with all knowledge, and able also to admonish one another. (Rom. 15:14)

> Brethren, even if a man is caught in any trespass, you who are spiritual, restore such a one in a spirit of gentleness. . . . Bear one another's burdens. (Gal. 6:1–2)

In violation of Scripture and to the spiritual detriment of themselves and others, Euodia and Syntyche had apparently refused to seek biblical counsel from those whom God had gifted and equipped to provide such help. Unfortunately, many Christians today are following their example. They will not seek a solution to their personal problems through the God-ordained means of counsel from pastors, elders, and other mature Christians. As a result, their conflicts become more serious, their testimony becomes more ineffective, and their joy and peace in Christ dissipates.

When you struggle with interpersonal problems and are not able to overcome them on your own, ask for help from your church leaders or other believers who you know will be able to counsel both you and the other person. Let them help you to biblically diagnose the causes of the conflict and find God's way of resolving it. Don't try to carry such a heavy burden by yourself, but allow others to receive the blessing of being peacemakers (Matt. 5:9).

Provide Help for Others

Another way that you can preserve and promote unity in the body is to be a peacemaker yourself. Pastors and other church leaders cannot counsel everyone in the church as extensively as they would like, so they need the help of members who can come alongside people who are caught in a conflict. That is why the New Testament commands to admonish and restore are given to the body as a whole and not just to leaders. If you are a Christian, those commands are given to you.

But you might say, "How can I counsel people when I have no formal training in psychology or theology?" First, no training in secular theories of psychology is necessary to help others in their spiritual lives, because God has declared that His Word and Spirit are sufficient for "everything pertaining to life and godliness" (2 Peter 1:3); "All Scripture is inspired by God. . . that the man of God may be adequate, equipped for every good work" (2 Tim. 3:16–17). In fact, secular psychological theory is so often contrary to the truth of Scripture that a knowledge of it can be detrimental to the task of helping people spiritually.[4] And regarding theology, even Christians without formal theological training know enough Scripture and have experienced enough of the Christian life to impart to others the truths they have learned. There is always someone who knows less than you in some area, and there is always someone struggling in an area where you have experienced some victory.

According to Romans 15:14, all true Christians are "competent to counsel" because they have been given all kinds of goodness and knowledge by the grace of God in Christ. But that does not mean you cannot grow in your ability to help others. In fact, you should be constantly growing in personal godliness and understanding of Scripture so that you can be a better example to others and teach them the truths that you learn. You can also study the specific biblical doctrines and practices that relate to counseling by reading good books on the subject and even receiving professional training that is available to laypeople.[5]

THERE IS HOPE

Our study of Philippians 4:2–3 has provided us with three important principles for preserving unity in a church body: we must recognize mutual responsibility in conflict, develop the mind of Christ toward others, and work together as a group of believers to resolve conflict. But in conclusion it would also be helpful to note something that Paul did *not* say to the Philippians. Though the conflict between Euodia and Syntyche was a serious one, Paul did not even imply that the situation might be irreparable or that one of the women might have to leave the church.

He did not say, "It's evident that you two women are incompatible. Euodia is an extrovert, and Syntyche is an introvert. Euodia is happy-go-lucky, and Syntyche is serious. Your backgrounds and personalities are just too different. Your ways of doing things are too diverse, and the problem has existed too long. My counsel, therefore, is that both of you should go your separate ways." Instead, Paul urged both women to work on solving the problem, implying that there was hope that the relationship could be repaired.

On another occasion, Paul wrote, "No temptation [or trial] has overtaken you but such as is common to man, and God is faithful, who will not allow you to be tempted beyond what you are able, but with the temptation will provide the way of escape also, that you may be able to endure it" (1 Cor. 10:13). Applied to interpersonal conflicts, that verse means that any two people who truly want to solve their problems can do so by the grace and power of God.

There is no problem that God cannot solve. The things that are impossible with men are possible with God (Matt. 19:26). No situation is hopeless or beyond repair—wounds can be healed, friendships can be restored, relationships can be cemented—when two people will handle their problems God's way. When Paul counseled Euodia and Syntyche and the rest of the Philippians, he made this very clear. He was actually echoing one of the important aspects of Christ's High Priestly Prayer in John 17. In that prayer, our Lord showed us the importance of unity and also provided us with the hope that we can indeed preserve it in the body. He prayed to the Father on behalf of all who believe in Him, "that they may be one, just as We are one; I in them, and Thou in Me, that they may be perfected in unity, that the world may know that Thou didst send Me" (John 17:22–23).

QUESTIONS FOR DISCUSSION AND APPLICATION

1. What are some reasons why inaction is an inappropriate response to conflict that arises in the body? What usually happens when we do nothing, and why?

2. How can two people disagree with one another but still be "of the same mind"? Give an example of that kind of relationship.

3. What kind of person should you go to for help when you have an interpersonal conflict? List some characteristics of a good "peacemaker."

4. What would you say to someone who is planning to leave the church because of complaints they have against someone else in the body?

10

PRAYING FOR ONE ANOTHER

One day Jesus' disciples came to Him and said, "Lord, teach us to pray" (Luke 11:1). They sensed the inadequacy of their own prayer lives and asked Jesus for instruction. Many Christians today feel a similar lack of confidence in their patterns of prayer. Very few of us could say that we need little or no improvement in this area of our lives. Inasmuch as many of us share the disciples' desire for instruction in prayer, we should be excited to know that we have been given far more instruction than they received from Christ on that day. We not only have His teaching recorded for us, but we also have the entire New Testament, which is filled with additional help for one who desires to know how to pray in a manner that glorifies God.

Second Timothy 3:16–17 says that the Word of God is able to make us "adequate, equipped for every good work." Certainly one of those good works is praying for the body of Christ as a whole and its members in particular, and in the Word we find examples of such prayers to instruct us. The apostle Paul often recorded in his letters the content of his prayers for the churches, and part of his purpose for doing so was that his readers might learn from his example how to pray for one another. Because his prayers are recorded in inspired Scripture, we know that they can serve as a model for us as we pray for our churches. It would be helpful to study all such prayers of Paul in depth, but in this chapter we will look primarily at one representative sample and seek to understand some guiding principles for our prayers concerning the body. That prayer is found in Ephesians 1:15–19.[1]

> For this reason I too, having heard of the faith in the Lord Jesus which exists among you, and your love for all the saints, do not cease giving thanks for you, while making mention of you in my prayers; that the God of our Lord Jesus Christ, the Father of glory, may give to you a spirit of wisdom and of revelation in the knowledge of Him. I pray that the eyes of your heart may be enlightened, so that you may know what is the hope of His calling, what are the riches of the glory of His inheritance in the saints, and what is the surpassing greatness of His power toward us who believe.

PRAY FOR THE WHOLE BODY

A deeper look at this passage reveals that Paul did not only pray for those in the church whom he knew well, nor did he only pray for those who had great spiritual or physical needs. Those are the people whom we naturally tend to pray for the most, but Paul's example can help us to avoid the danger of imbalanced prayer that excludes some members of the body.

Paul Prayed for the Church as a Corporate Entity

It is biblical to encompass in prayer all the members of a particular group by praying for that group as a whole. This is because God works with groups of people as well as individuals personally. Romans 5:12–21 and other passages reveal that all mankind can be separated into two groups, each with a common headship and a shared relationship to God. One group, because of sin, remains "in Adam" and will continue in separation from God and reap eternal punishment. The other group is "in Christ," is justified through His death on the cross, and will enjoy Him forever in heaven. This second group is known as "the elect," "God's people," or "the church." It is the corporate, spiritual body that Christ prayed for in His High Priestly Prayer in John 17. He also continues to intercede in heaven for His body (Rom. 8:34; Heb. 7:25).

The Old Testament indicates that God has also related to earthly nations as corporate entities. Of course that was true of the people of Israel, all of whom were affected by the way God dealt with the nation as a whole (Deut. 5:32–6:3). But it was also true of the gentile nations, who would be blessed or cursed depending on how they treated Israel and her God (Gen. 12:3; 27:29). And it seems clear that to some degree in the New Testament era, God relates to individual local churches in this holistic fashion. Most of the epistles were written to churches as a whole, as were the messages from Christ in Revelation 2 and 3, which included warnings like this to a church: "Remember therefore from where you have fallen, and repent and do the deeds you did at first; or else I am coming to you, and will remove your lampstand out of its place—unless you repent" (Rev. 2:5).

The church who received that warning about corporate chastening was the church at Ephesus—the same one Paul was praying for in our passage. Undoubtedly he prayed for the church as a whole because he did not want it to be cursed in that way, but to be blessed. We as Christians today should also remember to pray for our church as a body, not only because we can benefit everyone in the church at one time through our prayer, but also because when we are thinking of the church as a *unit*, we will learn to think in ways that promote *unity* (cf. 1 Cor. 12:12–27).

Paul Prayed for Those Who Might Normally Be Neglected

When we pray for our church, we should not only pray generally for the body as a whole but also remember individuals in the church by name.[2] When we do that, however, we tend to pray primarily (or only) for certain kinds of people who come to mind. In his prayer, Paul refers by implication to some people about whom we may need to be reminded.

First, Paul prayed for *those who were not his close associates.* He says, "After I heard of your faith" (NKJV), which means that he had been away from the Ephesians long enough to be in need of a report on how they were doing. He had founded the church at Ephesus (Acts 19) but now was in prison and had not seen any of the members for several years. The church probably had many new people whom Paul had never met. Nonetheless, he prayed for these people who were strangers to him, or at least were not in his current circle of acquaintances (cf. 1 Thess. 3:5–10).

This is a strong contrast to our typical "out of sight, out of mind" mentality. We tend to think about and pray for our closest friends, or people involved in our personal ministries, or those whom we "run into" most often. But Paul's example should teach us to pray for those we only "hear about" or do not see regularly. That broadens our personal ministries, helps us to avoid cliquishness, and otherwise promotes unity in the body, as mentioned above.

Notice also that Paul prayed for *those who were spiritually prosperous.* He said he had heard "of the faith in the Lord Jesus which exists among you, and your love for all the saints." Many members of the Ephesian church were walking by faith and showing sacrificial love to all Christians without discrimination (even those in other cultures). These are marks of spiritual maturity and stability, and so some of us might think that Paul was wasting his time by praying for them when there were so many others trapped in sin and doctrinal error. Shouldn't we pray mainly for the especially "needy"? Not according to Paul. In fact, a study of his other prayers recorded in the New Testament reveals that he actually seems to have prayed more often for Christians who were succeeding spiritually. He did pray for people with problems, but he certainly did not take them off his prayer list when they had "conquered their problems" and were living in a manner pleasing to God.

One reason for this is that Paul knew there is always room for growth in any believer's life. None of us reaches perfection in this world. We trust Christ but not as much as we should. We love the saints but not nearly enough. We serve Christ, but nowhere to the extent that He deserves. We know some of the Word of God but none of us knows as much as we ought to. No church is as spiritual as it could be, and no individual Christian will reach the point in this life where he or she does not need our prayers any longer. On the contrary, it is dangerous to withhold prayer support from people simply because they are "doing well." First Corinthians 10:12 says, "Let him who thinks he stands take heed lest he fall."

How do you think the Notre Dame football team took a 24–0 lead over USC in 1972, only to lose 55–24? And how do you think the Buffalo Bills accomplished the greatest comeback in National Football League history in 1993 when they beat the Houston Oilers 41–38 after being behind 35–3 in the third quarter? Part of the answer must be that the Notre Dame and Houston players became overconfident with their big leads and relaxed their efforts enough to allow such debacles to occur.

Unfortunately, that kind of collapse can happen in the spiritual realm as well—in the lives of churches and their individual members. The history of the church at Ephesus itself is a testimony to that sad fact. Paul wrote in his letter that it exhibited great faith and a love for all the saints, but not many years later Jesus had to speak these words to the church: "I have this against you, that you have left your first love. Remember therefore from where you have fallen" (Rev. 2:4–5). And not only can churches or individuals lose their first love, but they can also fall hopelessly into a spiritual deadness or even an outright denial of Christ (Rev. 3:14–18; cf. Demas in Philem. 24 and 2 Tim. 4:10).[3]

That danger should motivate us to pray fervently not only for churches and individual members who are in the midst of crises, but also for those who are prospering spiritually. They can lose their enthusiasm, their stability, and their commitment to Jesus Christ and His truth. But through our prayers, God can deliver them from such a fate and grant them His continued blessing (cf. 1 Cor. 1:11).

PRAY WITHOUT CEASING

Paul told the Ephesians that he *did not cease* giving thanks for them or making mention of them in his prayers. He was fulfilling the command that he gave in 1 Thessalonians 5:17 to "pray without ceasing," and we should too when we pray for our brothers and sisters in Christ. But what does that command mean? Does it mean that we should never do anything else but pray? Does it mean that we must somehow pray during every other thought and activity we experience? No, that was not what "pray without ceasing" meant to Paul. Rather the command included the ideas of praying frequently, never abandoning prayer, and being quick to go to prayer.

We Should Pray Frequently

Our lives as Christians should be characterized by prayer. We should pray so often that each of us could be described as "always praying." Prayer should not be a merely occasional occurrence. We are commanded to follow the example of our Lord Jesus Christ (1 John 2:6), and He was a man of constant and regular prayer.

Luke 22:39 tells us that after the Last Supper Jesus "came out and proceeded *as was His custom* to the Mount of Olives." He was going there to pray, of course. Times of prayer were customary in Christ's life, because He carried out a regular schedule of daily prayers as any devout Jew would. New Testament scholar Joachim Jeremias, in his book *The Prayers of Jesus,* says that "Jesus came from a people who knew how to pray." He goes on to discuss the historical evidence for the practice of ritual prayer by the Jews in the days of Christ.[4] He concludes that discussion by saying,

> Thus we see that sunrise, afternoon (3 p.m.) and sunset were the three daily times of prayer for the Jews of the New Testament era. In the morning and in the evening, they would recite the *Shema*, framed by benedictions and followed by the *Tephilla*, in the afternoon the latter was prayed alone. These three hours of prayer, together with the benedictions said before and after meals, were Israel's great treasure, the skeleton framework for an education in prayer and for the practice of prayer for everyone from their youth upwards."[5]

Jesus almost certainly practiced those times of prayer each day: He was raised in a devout home (Luke 2:21ff.; 4:16). Scripture mentions Him praying at those times (Mark 1:35; 6:46–47). And His teaching contains references to that practice (cf. Luke 10:26; 18:9–14). Jeremias says that "we may conclude with all probability that no day in the life of Jesus passed without the three times of prayer: the morning prayer at sunrise, the afternoon prayer at the time when the afternoon sacrifice was offered in the temple, the evening prayer at night before going to sleep."[6] But those were not the only times Jesus spent in prayer. Scripture contains examples of His erupting in spontaneous prayers throughout His ministry (Matt. 11:25–26; John 11:41–42), as well as offering longer prayers at odd hours, such as the High Priestly Prayer in John 17 and His time in the Garden of Gethsemane.

Since God's plan for us is that we be "conformed to the image of His Son" (Rom. 8:29), we know we should please God by offering prayer to Him frequently and regularly. And in those times of prayer we should make sure to remember "the church of God which He purchased with His own blood" (Acts 20:28).

We Should Never Stop Praying

Another way in which we can fulfill the command to "pray without ceasing" is to continue in prayer for the church and its members even in the times when we are tempted to abandon prayer. When Paul said that he did not cease praying for his fellow believers, he meant that he never gave up on prayer. He did not stop praying for people who were spiritually prosperous, as previously noted; nor did he stop praying for those who had rejected his counsel or fallen into sin. He never said, "There's no use praying for them; they're too far gone," "I might as well stop praying because I'm not getting through anyway," or even "My heart is too cold or my own sin too great to pray." Rather than causing us to stop praying, such concerns should stimulate us to pray even more.

The following quotes from Charles Spurgeon are helpful in this regard:

As we breathe without ceasing, so must we pray without ceasing. As there is no attainment in life, of health, or of strength, or of muscular vigor which can place a man beyond the necessity of breathing, so no condition of spiritual growth or advance in grace will allow a man to dispense with prayer. . . .

Never give up praying, not even though Satan should suggest to you that it is in vain for you to cry unto God. Pray in his teeth; "pray without ceasing." If for awhile the heavens are as brass and your prayer only echoes in thunder above your head, pray on; if month after month your prayer appears to have miscarried, and no reply has been vouchsafed to you, yet still continue to draw nigh unto the Lord. Do not abandon the mercy-seat for any reason whatever. If it be a good thing that you have been asking for, and you are sure it is according to the divine will, if the vision tarry wait for it, pray, weep, entreat, wrestle, agonise till you get that which you are praying for. If your heart be cold in prayer, do not restrain prayer until your heart warms, but pray your soul unto heat by the help of the everblessed Spirit who helpeth our infirmities. If the iron be hot then hammer it, and if it be cold hammer it till you heat it. Never cease prayer for any sort of reason or argument. If the philosopher should tell you that every event is fixed, and, therefore, prayer cannot possibly change anything, and, consequently, must be folly; still, if you cannot answer him and are somewhat puzzled, go on with your supplications notwithstanding all. No difficult problem concerning digestion would prevent your eating, for the result justifies the practice, and so no quibble should make us cease prayer, for the assured success of it commends it to us. You know what your God has told you, and if you cannot reply to every difficulty which man can suggest, resolve to be obedient to the divine will, and still

"Pray without ceasing." Never, never, never renounce the habit of prayer, or your confidence in its power.[7]

We Should Be Quick to Go to Prayer

A third application of the command to "pray without ceasing" is that we should instinctively turn to our heavenly Father many times in our daily lives. We should immediately respond to the events that occur in our daily lives, whether they are good or bad, with thanksgiving (1 Thess. 5:18) and petition (Eph. 6:18). Jesus was known to break into prayer in response to everyday events, as mentioned before; Paul would offer spontaneous prayers to God even in the midst of writing his epistles (Rom. 11:33–36; 15:5, 13, 33); and the Old Testament saint Nehemiah repeatedly spoke to God during his work on the walls of Jerusalem.

Likewise, the ebb and flow of our daily lives should be filled with brief prayers that are our first response to the situations we face. We ought to be lifting our hearts to our Father throughout the day, saying, "Lord, help me to glorify You. Lord, teach me. Lord, guide me. Lord, open doors of opportunity. Lord, deliver me from evil. Lord, watch over my eyes. Lord, you know that person can upset me, so please help me. Lord, give me wisdom. Lord, I am thinking of a certain person right now. He just came to my mind, and I know he has some needs. Please help him. Thank you for protecting me just now," and so on. Wherever we are or whatever we may be doing, we should pray about anything or anyone that comes to mind.

Is prayer your initial response to situations that arise in the church? It should be. When a conflict begins to brew or has exploded into a war, you should pray alone about it and pray with some others who know about it or are involved in it. When you hear that the church is facing a financial problem,

222

that should immediately be put on your prayer list and you should inquire into opportunities for corporate prayer about the issue. If you become concerned about something in your pastor's life or teaching, you should pray for him repeatedly before you talk with him or others about the problem. Only when the members of a church "pray without ceasing" will it be the kind of body that honors the Lord.

PRAY WITH THANKSGIVING

In Ephesians 1:15–16, Paul says, "I . . . do not cease *giving thanks for you.*" His prayers for the Ephesians and for the other churches were filled with thanksgiving to God. Again, he was practicing what he preached, because throughout his epistles he commands Christians to give thanks (Phil. 4:6; Col. 4:2; 1 Tim. 2:1; etc.). Notice, however, that Paul is specifically giving thanks for the people of God in this particular congregation, something that he does in most of his epistles.[8] And in most cases, he does this *before* he goes on to make petitions to God regarding their spiritual welfare or problems in their midst. We would do well to follow his example when we pray for our churches, for a number of reasons.

First, regularly giving thanks for the people in our congregations will help us to have a humble mind set that promotes service for others. Philippians 2:1–3 says that a motivation for esteeming others as more important than ourselves is the fact that in the body we have a common "encouragement in Christ," "consolation of love," and "fellowship of the Spirit" (v. 1). When you think of what God has done in the lives of people in your church and thank Him for that work, you will focus more on others rather than yourself and become more eager to participate in God's work by serving others in the body.

Second, thanking God for others in the church reminds us that it is He who has placed each member in the body, according to His divine will. This will help us to avoid attitudes that might engender conflict or division in the body, because we will realize that it is God Himself who put us together in the same body for His good purposes. If you feel anger or dissatisfaction because certain people are a part of your church, then your problem is really with God rather than those people. In His divine wisdom He knew that it was best for you to be co-members with those people, so it would be to your benefit to stop fighting His plan and be open to what He wants you to learn from the others in the diverse society of the church.

In 1 Corinthians 12, a passage discussing spiritual gifts in the body of Christ, God in His three persons is referred to twenty-two times, and most of those references are specifically for the purpose of emphasizing that He is the One who has constituted the body "just as He wills" (v. 11) or "just as He desired" (v. 18). Paul wrote this letter to the Corinthians largely to eliminate the divisions among them (cf. 1 Cor. 1:11–13; 3:3–5). He wanted them to understand that their differing gifts, personalities, and even approaches to ministry were all a part of God's sovereign plan for the church. He writes, "God has so composed the body . . . that there should be no division in the body, but that the members should have the same care for one another. And if one member suffers, all the members suffer with it; if one member is honored, all the members rejoice with it. Now you are Christ's body, and individually members of it" (1 Cor. 12:24–27).

A third reason for giving thanks to God for the people in our church is that it helps us to think of the good things about them and the positive work God is doing in their lives, rather than merely thinking and praying about the problems that arise. Any church could be considered a bad church if we looked only at its "negatives," but any biblical church should also inspire gratefulness in us when we think about the ways in which God is building the church (Matt. 16:18). Anywhere there are true believers, God is at work and should be praised for His graciousness. Focusing on the positive characteristics of other individual members also helps promote unity in the body, because it is hard to be sinfully critical of people for whom we are regularly giving thanks.

Ephesians 1:15 tells us what Paul was thankful for in the lives of that church. He gave thanks unceasingly for their *faith* and for their *love*. These spiritual realities were the focus of his gratefulness, not earthly considerations like the quality of their church building, the winsome personalities of the members, or the entertainment value of their worship services. Regardless of whether your church has such accouterments, you can thank God constantly for the faith and love He has produced in the body.

Pray About Spiritual Issues

Now that we understand our need to pray for the whole body of Christ in our local congregation, to pray without ceasing for that body, and to always express our gratefulness to God, we can discuss the content of Paul's prayer for the Ephesian church. Because the requests in Ephesians 1:15–19 are inspired by the Holy Spirit, they should serve as a model for us when we pray for our churches, both generally and specifically.

The general principle that is evident in this prayer of Paul, and all his other prayers for churches, is that he concerned himself almost exclusively with spiritual issues, rather than earthly or physical ones. We do not find him praying for things like Aunt Molly's sore big toe, the construction of Deacon Ben's in-ground pool, or even the deferred maintenance on the church campus. Certainly such earthly and physical needs are often legitimate subjects for prayer (cf. Phil. 4:6; James 5:13–16), but Paul's example teaches us that the *primary* focus of our prayers for the body should be the spiritual needs of its members and their effectiveness in ministry. Doing this will help us to overcome our fleshly tendency to focus too much on the temporal rather than the eternal (cf. 2 Cor. 4:18; Col. 3:2). It will also accomplish much more, because the foundational issues in people's lives are the spiritual ones, which affect their attitude toward their temporal situations. For instance, God may not take away Aunt Molly's sore toe, but He can give her the grace to glorify Him and be joyfully content even while she is suffering (Rom. 5:3–5; James 1:2–4), and use this trial to give her opportunities to reach out to others with the gospel and the love of God (2 Tim. 1:8, 2 Cor. 1:3–7). Praying for such things has been called "kingdom-oriented prayer."

Since we should focus on spiritual issues when we pray for the church, it would be helpful to know some specific petitions that please God and truly help people to grow in Christ. Paul's prayers in Ephesians 1 and elsewhere in the New Testament provide us with the examples we need. The next several pages contain his recorded prayers, each followed by a list of requests from that prayer (with the repetitions omitted). These lists should help you to see what kind of requests Paul presented to God for the churches, and also to provide a scriptural guide for you to use when you pray for your church. You might want to set aside a regular time to pray for your church body and read through this section, praying for each request as you go. The prayers are listed in order of their appearance in the New Testament, with the Ephesians 1 passage included.

Romans 1:8–12

> I thank my God through Jesus Christ for you all, because your faith is being proclaimed throughout the whole world. For God, whom I serve in my spirit in the preaching of the gospel of His Son, is my witness as to how unceasingly I make mention of you, always in my prayers making request, if perhaps now at last by the will of God I may succeed in coming to you. For I long to see you in order that I may impart some spiritual gift to you, that you may be established; that is, that I may be encouraged together with you while among you, each of us by the other's faith, both yours and mine.

- Pray that your church will have a ministry beyond the community in which it is located. Remember some specific missionaries or members serving in other areas.
- Pray that you personally will be able to build relationships in the body in which you can help others to grow in Christ and serve Him better. Mention some believers with whom you already have relationships, and pray about some specific ways you can build them up spiritually.
- Pray that you and the other members of the church will find encouragement in Christ by sharing with one another the good things God is doing in your lives. Ask God to help you and others not to focus primarily on the weaknesses of the body and its members, but rather on the common faith that you all share.

Ephesians 1:16–19

> [I] do not cease giving thanks for you, while making mention of you in my prayers; that the God of our Lord Jesus Christ, the Father of glory, may give to you a spirit of wisdom and of revelation in the knowledge of Him. I pray that the eyes of your heart may be enlightened, so that you may know what is the hope of His calling, what are the riches of the glory of His inheritance in the saints, and what is the surpassing greatness of His power toward us who believe.

- Pray that each member would have a spirit that is teachable and receptive to what God is saying through His Word. Think of those especially who need wisdom and guidance from the Word for important decisions in their lives.
- Pray that through the teaching of the church and personal study, the members of your church body would understand that God has given them "every spiritual blessing in the heavenly places" (Eph. 1:3) and be truly grateful to Him for His great love. Ask that God would specifically help them to realize that He has sovereignly called them to Himself because of His eternal choice, that a blissful future awaits them in heaven, and that even now God is causing "all things to work together for good" in their lives (Rom. 8:28).

Ephesians 3:14–21

> For this reason, I bow my knees before the Father, from whom every family in heaven and on earth derives its name, that He would grant you, according to the riches of His glory, to be strengthened with power through His Spirit in

the inner man; so that Christ may dwell in your hearts through faith; and that you, being rooted and grounded in love, may be able to comprehend with all the saints what is the breadth and length and height and depth, and to know the love of Christ which surpasses knowledge, that you may be filled up to all the fulness of God. Now to Him who is able to do exceeding abundantly beyond all that we ask or think, according to the power that works within us, to Him be the glory in the church and in Christ Jesus to all generations forever and ever. Amen.

- Pray that God would give spiritual strength to the people in your church that would enable them to endure any trial with contentment and even joy. Specifically remember those who are going through a time of testing.
- Pray that love for one another would be a foundational commitment of everyone in your church, so that even the most extraordinary wind of conflict or difficulty could not "pull up the roots" of unity in the body.
- Pray that the awareness of Christ's great love for His people would be so strong in your church that the lives of all the members would reflect God's character and bring Him glory in this generation and in generations to come. Remember the families in which the next generation of believers are being trained and molded.

Philippians 1:9–11

And this I pray, that your love may abound still more and more in real knowledge and all discernment, so that you may approve the things that are excellent, in order to be sincere and blameless until the day of Christ; having been filled with the fruit of righteousness which comes through Jesus Christ, to the glory and praise of God.

- Pray that your love for one another in the body would always be growing, but that it also would never be a "love" that ignores the truth or fails to correct error. Also pray that any necessary confrontation would take place "in love" (Eph. 4:15).

- Pray for the holiness and purity of your church—that God would be pleased by the commitment to excellence in worship, teaching, and testimony; that there would be no reason for Christ to rebuke you as He did some of the churches in Revelation 2 and 3; and that your church would be known for its members' righteous lives. Thank God for those who are exemplary in their godliness, and mention those whose lives need to change. Pray also for God to use you in any way He can to help them (Gal. 6:1–2).

Colossians 1:9–12

> For this reason also, since the day we heard of it, we have not ceased to pray for you and to ask that you may be filled with the knowledge of His will in all spiritual wisdom and understanding, so that you may walk in a manner worthy of the Lord, to please Him in all respects, bearing fruit in every good work and increasing in the knowledge of God; strengthened with all power, according to His glorious might, for the attaining of all steadfastness and patience; joyously giving thanks to the Father, who has qualified us to share in the inheritance of the saints in light.

- Pray that the people in your church would study God's revealed will in the Scriptures and learn how to apply the Word to every part of their lives. Ask God to make them "doers of the Word, and not merely hearers who delude themselves" (James 1:22).

- Pray that they would have the inner strength through the Spirit of God to persevere in faith and godliness throughout all the twists and turns of life. Pray specifically for anyone you know who has considered "giving up."
- Ask God to produce a true joy and gratefulness in your church body, so that a cynical or critical spirit could never creep in and cause coldness or division.

Those are some of the spiritual issues we can pray about when we intercede for our churches. We can know that God will work among us if we pray for these things in the manner we have discussed in this chapter.

The greatest need of our churches today is not for profound theologians or powerful preachers or other resources, though they are necessary and helpful. The greatest need is for people who will *pray* biblically, unceasingly, and powerfully. James 5:16 says that "the effective prayer of a righteous man can accomplish much." A church may not have the next Spurgeon in its pulpit and it may lack many resources for ministry, but if its people pray, it will be effective. Satan trembles when even the weakest saint is on his knees before God.

The spiritual battles for the souls of men, women, and children are not won when the preacher comes into the pulpit or the evangelist hits the streets. They are won before the preaching or evangelism even starts, by the people who come before the throne of God in prayer. It is *God* who does the work of convicting, regenerating, converting, sanctifying, empowering, and protecting—and He does more of that work when His people pray. That is not to imply, of course, that God changes His plan in response to our prayers, but that

God uses prayer as a means to accomplish His plan (cf. John 15:16; 1 John 5:14). That is precisely why we can have such confidence that God will bless our churches when we are faithful in prayer for them, and also why we are the ones to blame when we do not pray and our churches go astray.

The prophet Samuel understood these truths when he said these words to the people of Israel: "The Lord will not abandon His people on account of His great name, because the Lord has been pleased to make you a people for Himself. Moreover, as for me, far be it from me that I should sin against the Lord by ceasing to pray for you" (1 Sam. 12:22–23).

QUESTIONS FOR DISCUSSION AND APPLICATION

1. Look back over the types of people that Paul prayed for, mentioned on pages 214–18. Do you tend to neglect any of those types of people in your prayers? Are there any other types of people you tend to neglect?

2. Review what it means to "pray without ceasing" and compare it to your own habits of prayer.

3. Imagine you are leading the prayer time in a small group, and someone asks for prayer regarding a sick pet. How could you respond to the request and guide the group into "kingdom-oriented prayer" (without offending the person with the pet)?

4. Pick one of the New Testament prayers discussed in the last pages of this chapter, and use the words in it to pray for your church. If you are meeting with a small group, use all of the passages in a time of prayer for your church.

CONCLUSION: THE HEART OF THE MATTER

In this book we have learned about important duties like committing ourselves to membership in a church, submitting to leadership, worshiping the Lord with His people, confronting one another in love, and praying for the body. What we have not addressed sufficiently, however, is the *reason* we should want to fulfill these duties, or the *motivation* by which we can find joy in doing what the Lord commands. But if we do all the right things for the wrong reasons, or because of motivations that are not pleasing to God, then all our labors are in vain. The Lord cares even more about what is happening in our hearts than what we are doing with our bodies or saying with our lips. So this conclusion is not a mere addendum to this book, but a necessary part of any discussion of our life in the Father's house.

First, when you strive to be a good member of a local church, you should do it *not to be saved, but because you have been saved.* Ephesians 2:8–9 says, "By grace you have been saved through faith; and that not of yourselves, it is the gift of God; not as a result of works, that no one should boast. For we are His workmanship, created in Christ Jesus for good works, which God prepared beforehand, that we should walk in them."

Notice the order of the thoughts in that passage: Salvation starts with the grace of God—a unilateral choice on His part to bestow unmerited favor on sinners who deserve only judgment (see Eph. 1:3–14, 2:1–7). The salvation that He has chosen to freely give us is received through faith, which means a complete reliance on the Person and work of Jesus Christ for the forgiveness of our sins (Rom. 3:21–26, 10:1–17). We clearly do *not* receive this salvation "as a result of works"—it is not based in any way on who we are or what we do (Luke 18:9–14, Titus 3:5). The change in our lives ("we are His workmanship") and the good works that we do ("which God prepared beforehand") are a *result* of our salvation, not the cause of it.

If you have read this far in the book, you obviously have an interest of some kind in being a good member of a church. But if you have been reading it with a "works-salvation" mentality, then the first thing you need to do is repent from trying to save yourself and ask the Lord to save you. Only by faith in Christ can you be a true member of His body and enjoy fellowship with Him and His people for all eternity.

Second, you should live your life in the Father's house *not to be more loved by God, but because He already loves you.* Romans 5:6–10 says,

> For while we were still helpless, at the right time Christ died for the ungodly. For one will hardly die for a righteous man; though perhaps for the good man someone would dare even to die. But God demonstrates His own love toward us, in that while we were yet sinners, Christ died for us. Much more then, having now been justified by His blood, we shall be saved from the wrath of God through Him. For if while we were enemies, we were reconciled to God through the death of His Son, much more, having been reconciled, we shall be saved by His life.

There is a clear progression of thoughts in that passage also. Paul says that prior to our salvation we were "helpless," "ungodly," "sinners," and "enemies" of God. At the time Christ died on the cross, we were "helpless" to save ourselves, because we would come into the world as a part of a fallen race that ever since Adam has been dead in our trespasses and sins (Eph. 2:1; cf. Gen. 2:16–17; Rom. 5:12). But we also would be "ungodly" when we came into the world, because our inherent nature would be to suppress the truth about God and His righteousness (Rom. 1:18–20). In short, we would all from birth fit the description that Jesus gave to the Pharisees when He said, "You are of your father the devil" (John 8:44; cf. Ps. 51:5). On top of that, we would become "sinners" in deed as well as in nature, choosing time and time again, from the earliest of our choices, to disobey the commands of God. As Romans 3:23 says, "All have sinned and fall short of the glory of God." And finally, the result of our sinful nature, and our actual sins, is that we were "enemies" of God—His holiness and justice demanded that He be against us, not for us. But because of Christ, we can now say with Paul, "If God is for us, who is against us?" (Rom. 8:31).

The good news is that because of what Christ did for us (long before we were born), we can now be united with Him through faith, and by being one with Him we can receive all the love that God the Father has for God the Son. And this love that the Father has for the Son, which we enjoy in Christ, will never fluctuate, waver, diminish, or cease throughout all eternity. It is an infinite love that will remain infinitely! So we do not, by our good works, cause God to love us more, nor do we cause Him to love us less by our bad works. Even when He disciplines us, He does so because He loves us, and wants us to share in His holiness (Heb. 12:5–11). The good works that we do in the church, therefore, should be motivated by a gratefulness to God for this great love He has bestowed upon us in His Son.

Third, the right motivation for your worship and ministry is not to be accepted or esteemed by others, but to be pleasing to God. Matthew 6:1–6 says,

> Beware of practicing your righteousness before men to be noticed by them; otherwise you have no reward with your Father who is in heaven. When therefore you give alms, do not sound a trumpet before you, as the hypocrites do in the synagogues and in the streets, that they may be honored by men. Truly I say to you, they have their reward in full. But when you give alms, do not let your left hand know what your right hand is doing that your alms may be in secret; and your Father who sees in secret will repay you. And when you pray, you are not to be as the hypocrites; for they love to stand and pray in the synagogues and on the street corners, in order to be seen by men. Truly I say to you, they have their reward in full. But you, when you pray, go into your inner room, and when you have shut your door, pray to your Father who is in secret, and your Father who sees in secret will repay you.

Some people in churches today are like the Pharisees—they attend because they want to be thought of as moral people with integrity, or as good parents for taking their children to church faithfully. Some others believe that faithful church attendance and service is good for their business, because people will be more likely to trust them. Whatever the motive may be, it is not a right one unless it is directed at pleasing God rather than men. The Lord is the only Person that we should be trying to impress. As 1 Corinthians 10:31 says, "Whether, then, you eat or drink or whatever you do, do all to the glory of God." And 2 Corinthians 5:9 says, "We have as our ambition . . . to be pleasing to Him."

Finally, you should not be involved in a church *to be served (primarily)*, *but to serve others in the name of Christ.* Mark 10:45 says, "For even the Son of Man did not come to be served, but to serve, and to give His life a ransom for many." Being a faithful member of a good church will certainly be a blessing to you personally, but that should not be your primary motive. In fact, you will be much more blessed when your primary goal is to be a blessing to others.

Some people serve in the music ministry basically because they enjoy playing their instrument on Sundays, or singing in the choir. So if they are not allowed to do it for some reason, they get upset. Others are "social animals" who love being in a crowd, hearing the latest gossip, or checking out what people are wearing—their reasons for going to church are not that much different from the reasons people go to parties or other social occasions. And so if they don't feel that they are being liked or noticed, they no longer have a reason to attend that church. But when we are motivated by a desire to serve God by serving His people, than any church, no matter what shape it is in, can be an exciting place to be. There is always someone there that we can serve—maybe especially when the church is not doing so well!

So as you go about living your life in the Father's house, be constantly examining your motives to see whether you are doing so out of gratefulness to the Lord who has loved you and saved you, and for the purpose of serving Him and others, rather than yourself. If you desire to be the best church member you can be, remember that the heart of the matter is the matter of the heart!

APPENDIX: MORE QUESTIONS FOR STUDY AND DISCUSSION

These additional questions are provided for use in small groups as homework assignments or review questions, or simply to assist individuals as they seek to digest and retain the material from this book.

Chapter 1: Realizing the Importance of the Local Church

1. What happened during the 1960s and 1970s that redirected the focus of people away from the church?

2. What is the good news and bad news about the church from the 1980s and 1990s?

3. How does the attitude toward the church expressed in the book *Exit Interviews* compare with the views of Christian leaders from the past, such as Augustine, Luther, and Calvin?

4. What does the Word of God say about the importance of the church, the relationship between personal spiritual vitality and the local church?

5. What does the Bible mean when it says that the church is God's household, and what implications may we draw from this fact?

6. What truths are implied in the phrase "the church of the living God"?

7. What does the phrase "the pillar of the truth" mean, and what does it imply about the church? How does the church function as "the pillar of the truth"?

8. What does the phrase "the support of the truth" mean, and what does it imply about the church? In what ways does the church function as "the support of the truth"?

9. What relevance does the material in this chapter have for church leaders and church members?

10. In what ways do some churches and individual Christians violate these truths about the church?

11. How do the truths in this chapter apply to your life? Are there ways you should change and improve in your relation to the church?

Chapter 2: Committing Ourselves to Church Membership

1. What do you think about Jay Adams's statement about church discipline and church membership?

2. What are three biblical reasons why every believer should be a member of a church?

3. What truths about church membership do we learn from Hebrews 10:24–25?

4. What implications about church membership may we draw from the "one another" passages of the Bible?

5. What does R. B. Kuiper say is the connection between the invisible church and the visible church?

6. Respond to this statement: "While church membership is not a prerequisite of salvation, it is a necessary consequence of salvation."

7. What truths about church membership are taught in 1 Thessalonians 5:12–13 and Hebrews 13:17?

8. How does church membership help the elders of the church to better exercise their oversight?

9. Explain how "membership clarifies the difference between believers and unbelievers."

10. How does membership cause the visible church to better reflect the invisible church?

11. How is membership essential to an orderly administration of the church?

12. List and explain some of the benefits of church membership.

13. What practical relevance does the material in this chapter have for church leaders and church members?

14. In what ways do some churches and individual Christians violate these truths about the church?

15. How do the truths in this chapter apply to your life? Are there ways you should change and improve in your relation to the church?

Chapter 3: Choosing a Good Church

1. What are some unbiblical criteria that people use in determining which church to join?

2. What are the three primary marks of a "good church" discussed in this chapter?

3. What basic teachings should characterize the church a Christian should join?

4. Describe in some detail the manner of teaching that should be characteristic of the church a Christian should join.

5. What is the difference between giving the Bible titular authority and giving it functional authority?

6. What attitude toward God should characterize the people of a "good church"?

7. What criteria may be used to distinguish between a God-centered and a man-centered church?

8. What attitude will a "good church" have toward people?

9. How was this attitude manifest toward believers and unbelievers by the church in Jerusalem (Acts 2:42–47)?

10. Why would an understanding of the truths taught in this chapter be important for both the church leaders and church members?

11. In what ways do some churches and individual Christians violate these truths about the church?

12. How do the truths in this chapter apply to your life? Are there ways you should change and improve in your relation to the church?

Chapter 4: Relating to Church Leadership

1. What two unbiblical extremes or abuses are sometimes found among God's people in reference to church authority? How do these two extremes manifest or express themselves?

2. What, in general, does Hebrews 13:17 indicate about the way church members should regard and respond to the leaders of the church?

3. Discuss the specific practical implications the word "obey" has for church members in reference to their church leaders.

4. What wrong understandings or applications of Hebrews 13:17 might church members and leaders have?

5. What, in general, would qualify or limit the concept of "obedience" for church members and church leaders?

6. What specific criteria should church members use in determining whether or not they should obey their church leaders?

7. What other insights about the way church members should regard and relate to church leaders are implied by the word "submit" in Hebrews 13:17?

8. What additional perspectives does 1 Thessalonians 5:12–13 provide about the way God wants church members to regard and relate to church leaders?

9. Is it possible for a church member to disagree with and even disobey the leaders of the church without violating the commands of Hebrews 13:17 and 1 Thessalonians 5:12–13? If so, how?

10. Why is the exercise of and proper response to appropriate authority so important for Christians?

11. Hebrews 13:17 commands church members to relate to their leaders in a way that enables them to fulfill their ministry with joy and not grief. In what specific

ways may church members enable their leaders to truly enjoy their role in the body of Christ?

12. Why would an understanding of the truths taught in this chapter be important for both the church leaders and church members?

13. In what ways do some churches and individual Christians violate these truths about the church?

14. How do the truths in this chapter apply to your life? Are there ways you should change and improve in your relation to the church?

Chapter 5: Fulfilling Our Roles as Men and Women

1. What conclusions about the differences between men and women were presented in the *Time* magazine articles?

2. Why is such a consideration as this important for the church?

3. Identify the three primary roles God has given to men in the church and some passages that mention them.

4. In your opinion, why aren't more men rising to fulfill these God-given challenges and responsibilities? Why do men need to be commanded to fulfill these responsibilities?

5. If you are a man, which qualities listed for godly examples do you lack?

6. Why is it important that church leaders possess these qualities? What happens when men who lack these qualities are put into positions of leadership in the church?

7. If you are a man, which of the twenty-five biblical qualities for leadership do you find most evident or

most lacking in your life? Rate yourself on each of these qualities on a scale of 0–5.

8. How do modern-day feminists depict the traditional biblical perspective on the role of women? Why is the feminists' view a "straw man," a caricature of the truth?

9. Why is such a consideration as this important to the church?

10. What is meant by the statement that "the difference between men and women is not one of quality or ability, but of function"?

11. Identify the four roles God has given to women in the church and some passages that mention them.

12. In your opinion, why do many women resist and resent this perspective on the role of women in the church?

13. Make a list of the qualities (not functions or responsibilities, but virtues) either explicitly stated or implied as necessary for women to fulfill their God-given role and responsibilities. Also reflect on and include in your list important qualities suggested by Proverbs 31:11–31 and 1 Peter 3:1–6.

14. Why is it important for the church that Christian women possess these qualities? What happens in the home, the church, and the world when women lack these qualities?

15. If you are a woman, which of these biblical qualities do you see lacking in your life?

16. Why would an understanding of the truths taught in this chapter be important for both the church leaders and church members?

17. In what ways do some churches and individual Christians violate these truths about the church?

18. How do the truths in this chapter apply to your life? Are there ways you should change and improve in your relation to the church?

Chapter 6: Participating in Worship Services

1. What biblical truths indicate that the topic of this chapter is extremely important for Christians?

2. What is worship? Give a general definition of the nature and essence of true worship.

3. Identify, define, illustrate, and support biblically important factors of true worship.

4. How do many Christians seem to evaluate whether or not a church service has been a good one?

5. What practical implications does the fact that "the focus of true worship is on God" have for us as Christians?

6. What is meant by the statement that "the participants in true worship actively respond to God with their whole being"?

7. What are some of the reasons why people do not really participate in or benefit from the worship services of the church?

8. What is meant by the statement that "the right kind of participation in a worship service begins long before the actual service begins"? Identify, explain, illustrate, and support biblically what is involved in preparing for worship.

9. How would you answer the question, "If worship services should find their greatest appeal and benefit in the

revelation of God through the teaching of His Word, why does there seem to be such ineffectiveness and boredom generated by many preachers?"

10. Study the list of ten suggestions for profiting from the preaching of the Word of God, and identify which of them you think Christians are most prone to neglect. Which are *you* most prone to neglect?

11. In what ways can Christians participate in the worship services through prayer? How can Christians make the worship services of the church more effective, meaningful, and God-honoring through prayer?

12. The Bible indicates that singing is an important part of our worship. What twofold role should music play in the corporate worship of God?

13. How important is it for believers to participate in the ordinances of baptism and the Lord's Supper? Give biblical reasons for your answer.

14. What unbiblical attitudes and practices do some professing Christians have toward these ordinances of the church?

15. Why are baptism and salvation linked closely in some passages of the Bible? What does baptism mean or symbolize?

16. What does "the Lord's Supper" mean or symbolize?

17. Why can giving be considered a part of worship?

18. On what basis can it be said that the primary place that giving should take place is the local church?

19. If worship includes serving one another in the services, how can and should individual Christians worship God

through this activity? What implications does the fact that worship includes serving others have for our corporate worship?

20. Why would an understanding of the truths taught in this chapter be important for both the church leaders and church members? Are there ways you should change and improve in your relation to the church?

Chapter 7: Using Our Spiritual Gifts

1. Why is ignorance about spiritual gifts harmful?

2. Give a brief definition of spiritual gifts.

3. Why is it important for the church and individual Christians to remember that it is God who gives spiritual gifts to the church (His people)?

4. What important truths does the phrase "according to the measure of Christ's gift" (Eph. 4:7) convey?

5. What does it mean that "while each one of us is commanded to be a general practitioner, each of us is also required to be a specialist"?

6. Briefly describe the purpose(s) of spiritual gifts, and support your description with Scripture references.

7. This chapter states that "as a member of the church of Jesus Christ, you should always be asking yourself these two questions as you think about the purpose of spiritual gifts." What are these two questions, and why should Christians ask them?

8. According to the Bible, what happens when the members of a church ask themselves those questions and faithfully exercise their spiritual gifts in ministry?

9. According to Charles Spurgeon, what happens when Christians do not serve God with all their hearts? Do you agree?

10. List some of the ways in which you are serving Christ in His church.

11. What method have you used to decide where and how you would serve Christ in His church?

12. What counsel would you give to a person who asks you how to decide where and how he should serve Christ in His church? What should a Christian do to discern where and how he should focus his service for God in His church?

13. What is the point of the statement that "many churches are filled with people who approach church life as if they were at a ball game"?

14. How is every Christian "like a snowflake"?

15. What are the implications of this concept for the church and for individual Christians?

16. Why would an understanding of the truths taught in this chapter be important for both the church leaders and church members?

17. In what ways do some churches and individual Christians violate these truths about the church?

18. How do the truths in this chapter apply to your life? Are there ways you should change and improve in your relation to the church?

Chapter 8: Confronting One Another in Love

1. According to this chapter, what are the two primary concerns that Jesus Christ has for the church?

2. Why do some people find the practice described in this chapter repulsive? Do you agree or disagree? Give reasons and Scripture to support your answer.

3. What is conveyed by the fact that we are to confront a "brother"?

4. When should we and when should we not confront a "brother"?

5. When is it wrong and unloving to ignore the sins of another?

6. List and define each of the words used in this chapter to describe the manner in which we should confront another person about his or her sins. What should and shouldn't be done?

7. What are the potential benefits of loving confrontation?

8. What practice is prescribed by the words "bring in the troops"?

9. When should this practice of "bringing in the troops" be employed?

10. What roles should the "troops" fulfill?

11. Describe the kind of people who should make up the "troops." What are the three qualifications for being a part of this group?

12. What practice should be reserved and used as a "last resort" in the process of confrontation?

13. Delineate the factors that could be used to encourage repentance before the whole church is informed about an unrepentant sinner.

14. What biblical benefits may accrue from announcing the name of an unrepentant sinner to the whole church? Give scriptural support for this practice.

15. What should a Christian do if his church is unwilling to practice church discipline?

16. How would you answer someone who said of church discipline, "Jesus would never do that!"?

17. What does the Bible mean when it says that unrepentant sinners should be "delivered to Satan" (1 Cor. 5:5; 1 Tim. 1:20)?

18. Why are confrontation and church discipline the loving things to do?

19. Why would an understanding of the truths taught in this chapter be important for both the church leaders and church members? Are there ways you should change and improve in your relation to the church?

Chapter 9: Preserving Unity in the Body

1. Who were Euodia and Syntyche? Write down everything you know about them as individuals.

2. What lessons may we learn from the fact that these two ladies were in conflict with each other?

3. What must we do to avoid disunity in the church?

4. What happens when initial conflicts are not handled properly?

5. How does the radiator illustration relate to conflict resolution in churches?

6. What are some wrong ways of handling conflicts?

7. Why does Paul repeat the verb "urge" in reference to both Euodia and Syntyche?

8. Describe three ways that people often contribute to conflicts.

9. How does doing nothing often make a situation worse?

10. If you find yourself involved in a conflict in the church, what principle of conflict resolution does Matthew 7:1–5 illustrate?

11. What does being of the same mind (Phil. 4:2) have to do with conflict resolution? What does Paul mean when he tells Euodia and Syntyche to "be of the same mind" (NKJV)?

12. Describe and support biblically some of the practical ways in which we can exhibit a servant's attitude in our thinking.

13. Why is it true that "it is not always wrong to make a judgment about someone else in your mind; in fact, sometimes it is necessary to do so" (cf. 1 Cor. 5:12)?

14. According to this chapter, "Paul tells us that there are some things that we are unable to judge and therefore should not try to judge." What are these things which we are unable to judge?

15. How can we reverse the tendency to think the best of ourselves and the worst of others?

16. What considerations can help us to relate to others in a gracious manner?

17. How does the phrase "in the Lord" relate to this matter of maintaining unity and resolving conflicts in the church?

18. What principles for maintaining unity and resolving conflict are taught by Philippians 4:3? What other passages of Scripture teach the same truths?

19. What would you say to someone who says, "How can I counsel people when I have no formal training in psychology or theology?"?

20. Why would an understanding of the truths taught in this chapter be important for both the church leaders and church members?

21. In what ways do some churches and individual Christians violate these truths about the church?

22. How do the truths in this chapter apply to your life? Are there ways you should change and improve in your relation to the church?

Chapter 10: Praying for One Another

1. For whom did the apostle Paul pray and what relevance does this have to our prayers?

2. Why should we as Christians pray for the church as a whole?

3. What does the phrase "after I heard of your faith" tell us about Paul's prayer life, and what challenge does this bring to us for our prayer lives?

4. What does a study of Paul's prayers recorded in the New Testament indicate about the people for whom he most frequently prayed?

5. Why do you think Paul did this?

6. What did Paul mean when he said that he did not cease giving thanks for them or making mention of them in his prayers?

7. Why is it important for us to make it a practice to give thanks for fellow Christians?

8. What do Paul's prayers indicate about the issues that Paul was mainly concerned about in his prayers?

9. Using Paul's prayers in Romans 1:8–12; Ephesians 1:16–19; Ephesians 3:14–21; Philippians 1:9–11; and Colossians 1:9–12 as models, list the items mentioned in these prayers for which we should constantly be praying.

10. This chapter states that "the spiritual battles for the souls of men, women, and children are not won when the preacher comes into the pulpit or the evangelist hits the streets. They are won before the preaching or evangelism even starts, by the people who come before the throne of God in prayer." Support this statement with biblical promises or examples.

11. Study the prayer of Daniel in Daniel 9:1–19, and note everything you can learn about effective prayer from this passage.

12. Study the words of Samuel in 1 Samuel 12:20–25, and note everything you discover about the importance and nature of prayer.

13. Why would an understanding of the truths taught in this chapter be important for both the church leaders and church members?

14. How do the truths in this chapter apply to your life? Are there ways you should change and improve in your relation to the church?

NOTES

Chapter 1: Realizing the Importance of the Local Church

1. David Watson, *I Believe in the Church* (Grand Rapids: Eerdmans, 1978), 13.

2. For critiques of the modern church growth movement, see Os Guinness, *Dining With the Devil* (Grand Rapids: Baker, 1993); John MacArthur, *Ashamed of the Gospel* (Westchester, Ill.: Crossway, 1993); and G. A. Pritchard, *Willow Creek Seeker Services* (Grand Rapids: Baker, 1996).

3. William Hendricks, *Exit Interviews* (Chicago: Moody Press, 1993).

4. Ibid., 17–18.

5. Ibid., 19.

6. Ibid.

7. Ibid., 268 (emphasis his).

8. Ibid., 289.

9. Ibid., 295.

10. Ibid., 300.

11. George Barna, *Revolution* (Wheaton: Tyndale, 2005), 37.

12. Ibid, 129. Barna goes on to say, "I am called to be the Church," echoing an earlier discussion in his book where he teaches that "the Church" in Scripture is not "a specific type of religious organization or spiritual form" (p. 37). In other words, he believes that the hundreds of references to the church in the New Testament (Gk. *ekklesia)* are only referring to the people who believe in Christ, and never to an organized group of them that worships on Sundays! The problem with this, of course, lies

in all the verses discussed in the book you are reading that talk about the ordination of church leaders, obedience to church authority, church discipline, church membership, the sacraments of the church, etc. Barna does not discuss any of those verses in his book.

13. J. Pelikan and H. Lehmann, eds., *Luther's Works*, 55 vols. (Philadelphia: Fortress; St. Louis: Concordia, 1955), 21:127.

14. John Calvin, *Institutes of the Christian Religion*, trans. F. L. Battles (Philadelphia: Westminster Press, 1960), 2:1012.

15. Ibid., 1024.

16. Sadly, this is true of Roman Catholicism and all the contemporary cults such as Mormonism, Jehovah's Witnesses, and Christian Science.

17. R. B. Kuiper, *The Glorious Body of Christ* (Grand Rapids: Eerdmans, 1966), 112–13 (emphasis his).

18. Colin Brown, ed., *The New International Dictionary of New Testament Theology* (Grand Rapids: Zondervan, 1986), 1:661.

19. Robert Saucy, *The Church in God's Program* (Chicago: Moody Press, 1972), 7.

Chapter 2: Committing Ourselves to Church Membership

1. R. B. Kuiper, *The Glorious Body of Christ* (Grand Rapids: Eerdmans, 1966), 111–12.

2. Charles Spurgeon, *Spurgeon at His Best*, comp. Tom Carter (Grand Rapids: Baker, 1988), 33–34.

3. Some may claim that the elders of a church only have authority in matters specifically commanded in Scripture, but it seems quite unnecessary to have commands to submit to *them* if they are only enforcing what Scripture has already said. The fact is, for the church to function properly, leaders need to make many decisions about matters not addressed directly in Scripture (such as worship times, funds distribution, and musical styles).

4. Eric Lane, *Members of One Another* (London: Evangelical Press, 1968), 19.

5. "Oklahoma Supreme Court Ruling Addresses Several Key Issues; Guinn v. Church of Christ," P. 2d, *Church Law and Tax Report* 3, 5 (September/October), 1989.

6. Kuiper, *Glorious Body of Christ*, 29–30.

7. Spurgeon, *Spurgeon at His Best*, 33.

8. In many churches, when new members join, the congregation makes a vow to them after they affirm their commitment to the church. At one church, for instance, the pastor says to the whole body: "Will you, by the power of the Holy Spirit, seek to carry out your God-given responsibilities to those who are joining our church, exercising mutual care, stimulating growth in grace, holiness, and knowledge? Will you seek to 'lead the way' by your example in the areas of Christian living that are designed by God to bring glory to Himself through His church?" The congregation then says, "We will."

9. Lane, *Members of One Another*, 66.

Chapter 3: Choosing a Good Church

1. David B. Barrett, ed., *World Christian Encyclopedia: A Comparative Study of Churches and Religions in the Modern World, A.D. 1900–2000* (Nairobi, Kenya: Oxford University, 1982), v.

2. We believe this is also true of the practice of miraculous sign gifts, such as speaking in tongues and healing. For an in-depth discussion of that issue, see Victor Budgen, *The Charismatics and the Word of God*, 2nd ed. (Faverdale North, Darlington: Evangelical Press, 1989).

3. John MacArthur, *Shepherdology: A Master Plan for Church Leadership* (Panorama City, Calif.: The Master's Fellowship, 1989), 44–45.

4. In our consideration of churches, we must therefore eliminate many of the denominations and movements that call themselves "Christian," because they simply do not conform to the apostles' teaching. They either have subtracted from it by embracing liberal theology (as in the case of most mainline Protestant denominations),

or they have contradicted it by adding tradition or further "revelation" (which is true of the cults and Roman Catholicism). Such churches are not true churches at all, and Bible-believing Christians should not be a part of them.

5. John Calvin, *The Acts of the Apostles* (Grand Rapids: Eerdmans, 1965), 1:85. Calvin goes on to comment about the Roman Catholic Church: "It is easy to learn from this how frivolous is the boasting of the Papists when with gaping mouths they confidently thunder out the name of the Church, whereas they have most shamefully corrupted the entire teaching of the apostles. For if what they say be fairly examined, we shall find no sound part at all; it is for the most part as unlike the apostles' teaching as darkness from light. The rule of divine worship, which ought to be sought out of the Word of God alone, is among the Papists only compounded out of the superstitious inventions of men. They have transferred to the merits of works the hope of salvation which ought to have rested in Christ alone. The invocation of God is utterly polluted with innumerable profane ravings. Whatever is heard among them is either a distortion or an overturning of the apostles' doctrine."

6. F. F. Bruce, *The Book of the Acts*, The New International Commentary on the New Testament (Grand Rapids: Eerdmans, 1988), 73.

7. Peter Davids, *The First Epistle of Peter*, The New International Commentary on the New Testament (Grand Rapids: Eerdmans, 1990), 70.

8. For a critique of the use of psychology in Christian counseling, see John MacArthur, *Our Sufficiency in Christ* (Waco, Tex.: Word, 1991); and for information on a biblical model of counseling, see *Introduction to Biblical Counseling*, by MacArthur and Mack, et al. (Waco, Tex.: Word, 1994).

9. Because church discipline is so clearly commanded in Scripture and yet so infrequently practiced, it serves as an especially good test of the quality of any particular church (see 2 Cor. 2:9). Simply asking the church leaders if they practice church discipline will often reveal whether that church is worthy of further consideration.

10. We know that this was not comparable to communism because the Christians retained some property and possessions (Acts 4:37; 5:4; 12:12ff.) and because the qualifying phrase, "as anyone might have need," reveals that it was a selected sharing (see also Acts 4:34–35). As Calvin wrote, "Thus we may gather . . . that they brought forth their goods and held them in common only with the object of relieving immediate necessity" (Calvin, *Acts of the Apostles*, 88). Ernst Haenchen summarizes the meaning of the passage well: "Whenever there is a need of money for the poor of the congregation, one of the property-owners sells his piece of land or valuables, and the proceeds are given to the needy" (*The Acts of the Apostles* [Philadelphia: Westminster Press, 1965]), 192.

11. Cf. Deut. 15:4ff.; Pss. 12:5; 14:6; 40:17; Isa. 25:4; Mark 14:7; John 13:29; Rom. 15:26; James 1:27; 2:15–17; 1 John 3:17.

12. MacArthur, *Shepherdology*, 91–92.

13. Jay Adams, *Handbook of Church Discipline* (Grand Rapids: Zondervan, 1986), 103.

14. John Polhill, *Acts*, The New American Commentary, vol. 26 (Nashville: Broadman Press), 122.

Chapter 4: Relating to Church Leadership

1. Roger Beardmore, ed., *Shepherding God's Flock* (Harrisonburg, Va.: Sprinkle Publications, n.d.), 105–6.

2. For more about feelings and their role in decision making, see Dave Swavely, *Decisions, Decisions: How (and How Not) to Make Them* (Phillipsburg, N.J.: P&R, 2003); and for more about the conscience, see chapter 8 of his book *Who Are You to Judge: The Dangers of Judging and Legalism* (Phillipsburg, N.J.: P&R, 2005).

3. Commentator William Lane says that "a cognate term *ektikos*, which denotes a 'habitual readiness' to comply, is used in describing military subordination" (*Hebrews 9–13*, Word Biblical Commentary [Dallas: Word, 1991]), 554.

4. D. Edmond Hiebert, *1 and 2 Thessalonians* (Chicago: Moody Press, 1971), 247.

5. Ibid., 250.

6. Leon Morris, *The First and Second Epistles to the Thessalonians* (Grand Rapids: Eerdmans, 1959), 167.

7. Jay Adams, *Shepherding God's Flock* (Grand Rapids: Zondervan, 1975), 330–31. Of course, if the member and the leaders simply cannot "agree to disagree," then the only way to avoid conflict at that point would be for the member to find another church so that he or she would not be divisive in that one.

8. The clause actually does not contain an imperative verb, but its syntax in relation to the rest of the verse is so unconventional that most commentators agree that it must have been meant in an imperative sense. Even if they are incorrect, the clause would still mean that the *purpose* of our submissive relationship to leaders is that they will enjoy their ministry.

9. Quoted in *The Biblical Illustrator*, ed. Joseph Exell (Grand Rapids: Baker, 1961), 666–67.

10. John Brown, *Epistle to the Hebrews* (London: Banner of Truth, 1972), 710.

11. Adams, *Shepherding God's Flock*, 329.

12. Simon Kistemaker, *Exposition of the Epistle to the Hebrews*, New Testament Commentary (Grand Rapids: Baker, 1984), 427.

Chapter 5: Fulfilling Our Roles as Men and Women

1. Christine Gorman, "Sizing Up the Sexes," *Time* (January 20, 1992), 42.

2. Those who believe that women can be pastors and elders cite Old Testament examples like Miriam, who was called a "prophetess" (Ex. 15:20), and Deborah, who was a judge in Israel (Judg. 4). But prophecy was a supernatural gift, not a leadership position, and 1 Corinthians 11:5–13 says that any woman who prophesies must do so in a way that is clearly subject to male leadership. And in the case of Deborah, a careful look at the Scriptures reveals that her role as a "judge" was different in a number of ways from the men who filled that role (see the Piper and Grudem book men-

tioned in the next note, pp. 216–17). Besides that, the role of judge in Israel was not an ongoing position established by the law of God—it existed at a time of great sin and upheaval among the people of God (Judg. 17:6, 21:25; cf. Isa. 3:12). And as John Calvin wrote, "If any one bring forward, by way of objection, Deborah and others of the same class, of whom we read that they were at one time appointed by the command of God to govern the people of God, the answer is easy. Extraordinary acts done by God do not overturn the ordinary rules of government, by which he intended that we should be bound" (commentary on 1 Timothy 2:11–12).

3. For very helpful discussion about the importance of male leadership in the church, see John Piper and Wayne Grudem, eds., *Recovering Biblical Manhood and Womanhood* (Westchester, Ill.: Crossway, 1991).

4. Alexander Strauch, *Biblical Eldership* (Littleton, Colo.: Lewis and Roth, 1986), 187–88.

5. Some of the qualities are repeated in the three separate lists, of course, and they are counted as only one quality in our list. Also, "free from the love of money" is considered the same as "not fond of sordid gain"; "having children who believe," in our opinion, should be translated "having faithful children," and so we included that quality with "manages his household well"; and the same Greek word is translated "prudent" in 1 Timothy and "sensible" in Titus, and so that quality is only mentioned once in our list.

6. Patricia Aburdene and John Naisbitt, *Megatrends for Women* (New York: Fawcett Columbine, 1992), 119.

7. David Wells, *No Place for Truth: Whatever Happened to Evangelical Theology* (Grand Rapids: Eerdmans, 1993), 28–29. Quotes are from Philip Schaff, *America: A Sketch of its Political, Social, and Religious Character*, ed. Perry Miller (Cambridge, Mass.: Harvard University Press, 1961), 55–56.

8. See especially the book mentioned in note 2.

9. William Hendriksen, *Exposition of the Pastoral Epistles*, New Testament Commentary (Grand Rapids: Baker, 1957), 108–9.

10. R. L. Dabney, *Discussions: Evangelical and Theological Two* (London: The Banner of Truth, 1967), 96.

11. Alexander Strauch, *Using Your Home for Christ* (Littleton, Colo.: Lewis and Roth, 1988), back cover.

12. Dorothy Patterson, "The High Calling of Wife and Mother in Biblical Perspective," in Piper and Grudem, eds., *Recovering Biblical Manhood and Womanhood*, 365, 377.

Chapter 6: Participating in Worship Services

1. Quoted in Donald Whitney, *Spiritual Disciplines for the Christian Life* (Colorado Springs: NavPress, 1991), 89.

2. John MacArthur, *The Ultimate Priority* (Chicago: Moody Press, 1983), 2–3.

3. Whitney, *Spiritual Disciplines for the Christian Life*, 81–82.

4. John Piper, *Desiring God* (Portland, Ore.: Multnomah, 1986), 72–73.

5. From Charles Spurgeon, *Spurgeon at His Best*, comp. Tom Carter (Grand Rapids: Baker, 1988), 223–24.

6. Jay Adams, *A Consumer's Guide to Preaching* (Wheaton, Ill.: Victor, 1991), 7.

7. Spurgeon, *Spurgeon at His Best*, 158.

8. James Rosscup, in *Rediscovering Expository Preaching*, John MacArthur and The Master's Seminary Faculty (Dallas: Word, 1992), 82.

9. F. F. Bruce, *Acts*, New International Commentary on the New Testament (Grand Rapids: Eerdmans, 1988), 77.

10. First Peter 3:21 calls baptism an "appeal" or "pledge," terminology that suggests a transaction that would normally involve such witnesses.

11. Spurgeon, *Spurgeon at His Best*, 121.

12. Michael Card, *Immanuel: Reflections on the Life of Christ* (Nashville: Nelson, 1990), 145.

13. Whitney, *Spiritual Disciplines for the Christian Life*, 79–80.

Chapter 7: Using Our Spiritual Gifts

1. When the New Testament says that an individual has received "a gift," it may be referring to a package of *giftedness* that includes a blend of various gifts that have been given to the church as a whole. For instance, Timothy is said to have "a gift" in 1 Tim. 4:14 and 2 Tim. 1:6, but throughout the pastoral epistles, he is described as exercising giftedness in various areas, including teaching (2 Tim. 2:2), preaching (2 Tim. 4:2a), exhortation (2 Tim. 4:2b), and evangelism (2 Tim. 4:5). So it is possible that his "gift" was a composite of ministry capabilities that enabled him to fulfill a unique role in the body. Every individual Christian seems to be this kind of "spiritual snowflake" who can serve in a way that no one else can.

2. Paul Bayne, *An Exposition of Ephesians* (Wilmington: Sovereign Grace, 1959), 291–92.

3. Donald Whitney, *Spiritual Disciplines for the Christian Life* (Colorado Springs: NavPress, 1991), 94–95.

4. Charles Spurgeon, *Spurgeon at His Best*, comp. Tom Carter (Grand Rapids: Baker, 1988), 188.

5. For example: John Murray's commentary on Romans in the New International Commentary series (Eerdmans), and John MacArthur's commentary on Corinthians (Moody Press).

Chapter 8: Confronting One Another in Love

1. Bill Gothard, *Rediscovering a Forgotten Truth* (Institute in Basic Youth Conflicts, 1976), 1. While we would disagree with many other aspects of Bill Gothard's teaching, we share his passion for the truth of Matthew 18 and find his book helpful in practically applying that passage.

2. Some manuscripts add "against you," and it may be that Jesus was speaking primarily about interpersonal conflict (cf. the parallel passage in Luke 17:3–4). But because of the obscurity of the textual data and corresponding biblical principles, we believe that this process also represents the ideal way of dealing with sin that a be-

liever observes in another believer, regardless of whether the observer is directly affected by the sin (cf. Rom. 12:5; 1 Cor. 12:26).

3. New Testament passages that speak about this error of judging a "brother" are 1 Corinthians 4:5–6 and James 4:11–12.

4. We would also suggest that ideally this fellowship should involve baptism and church membership, because in the early church it is not likely that anyone would have been considered a "brother" without being baptized or joining the church. See the discussions about those issues in chapters 2 and 6, and also the discussion of what is a biblical church in chapter 3.

5. For an extensive discussion of the sin of judging and the problem of legalism, see Dave Swavely, *Who Are You to Judge? The Dangers of Judging and Legalism* (Phillipsburg, N.J.: P&R, 2005).

6. This seems also to be the meaning of the graciousness referred to in Eph. 4:32 and Col. 3:13.

7. Jay E. Adams, *From Forgiven to Forgiving* (Amityville, N.Y.: Calvary Press, 1994), 34.

8. This is not a psychological trick, but a biblical practice based on the approach of Paul in most of his epistles. Before he addressed the problems in each church, he thanked God for the good things in their midst (e.g., 1 Cor. 1:4–9).

9. If one person claims to have observed another sinning and the second party denies it, we believe that it would be prudent and loving for the "one or two more" to thoroughly investigate the claims of both people. This would, of course, include extended discussion with them and any other measures that might reveal their true characters and lifestyles (such as discreetly talking to their families or even visiting their homes). When such a fracture occurs between two believers, God is not pleased with either of them until it is healed (Matt. 5:23–24).

10. Jay E. Adams, *Handbook of Church Discipline* (Grand Rapids: Zondervan, 1986), 60.

11. Notice also that in 1 Tim. 5:19–20, it is Timothy (a church leader) who receives the accusation and then rebukes the sinner "in the presence of all."

12. The word "treat" seems to be more appropriate than "regard" or "consider," because it is hard to imagine that Jesus would condone the nasty attitude that Jews had toward Gentiles and tax-gatherers. He does want us to separate ourselves from a sinning brother, however, which corresponds with the actions of the Jews toward those people.

13. Some believers throughout history have practiced an extreme form of "shunning" in which people have even left their spouses because of church discipline. This is not in keeping with the spirit of Jesus' and Paul's instructions, which are designed to eliminate any form of *spiritual* fellowship from the lives of sinning brothers. A wife, for instance, can continue to fulfill her responsibilities of loving and submitting to her husband without affirming his sinful lifestyle in any way (cf. 1 Peter 3:1–2). And when Paul said "not even to eat with such a one," he was either referring to communion or speaking of withdrawing from one who is sinning while still in the church, prior to excommunication (cf. 2 Thess. 3:6–15).

14. John Calvin, *Institutes of the Christian Religion*, trans. Henry Beveridge (Grand Rapids: Eerdmans, 1979), 2:453.

Chapter 9: Preserving Unity in the Body

1. For information on when sin can be overlooked, see chapter 8, under the heading "What Sins Should We Confront?" It should be noted that the concept of overlooking or covering sin applies to situations where you have been offended. If you are the offender, on the other hand, and there is any possibility that the other person has taken offense, you should go to him to make sure no conflict develops. As we mature in Christ, we should be overlooking more and more sin against us, but going to our brothers more and more when we have offended them.

2. To learn more about the problem of judging and how you can avoid it, see Dave Swavely, *Who Are You to Judge? The Dangers of Judging and Legalism* (Phillipsburg, N.J.: P&R, 2005).

3. For an excellent practical discussion of forgiveness and other biblical principles for interpersonal relationships, read Jay E. Adams, *From Forgiven to Forgiving* (Amityville, N.Y.: Calvary Press, 1994). Wayne Mack, *Your Family, God's Way* (Phillipsburg, N.J.: Presbyterian and Reformed, 1990), in chapters 4–14, also provides helpful information for preventing and resolving conflicts. Kenneth Sande, *The Peacemaker* (Grand Rapids: Baker, 1991) is another excellent resource.

4. For critiques of the use of secular psychology by Christians, see John MacArthur, *Our Sufficiency in Christ* and *The Vanishing Conscience* (Word); Ed Bulkley, *Why Christians Can't Trust Psychology* (Word); and Richard Ganz, *Psychobabble* (Crossway).

5. Some helpful books to begin with are *Introduction to Biblical Counseling*, ed. John MacArthur and Wayne Mack (Word) and *Competent to Counsel* and *The Christian Counselor's Manual*, by Jay E. Adams (Zondervan). For information on training in biblical counseling, contact The Master's College, 21726 Placerita Cyn. Rd., Santa Clarita, CA 91321, www.masters.edu/contact, where Wayne Mack is an adjunct professor of biblical counseling. This college offers a full program of undergraduate and graduate studies in biblical counseling. Chapter 20 in the book *Introduction to Biblical Counseling* contains an extensive list and description of resources for biblical counseling.

Chapter 10: Praying for One Another

1. In addition to Eph. 1:15–19, Paul also reveals some of the content of his prayers in Rom. 1:8–12; 1 Cor. 1:4–9; Eph. 3:14–21; Phil. 1:3–11; Col. 1:3–12; 1 Thess. 1:2–3.

2. If you are a member of a small church, an ideal way for you to do this would be to use the members' list (or directory) and pray for every member on some kind of rotation plan. If your church is too big to do that realistically, then perhaps you could make a prayer list of various members according to the principles in this chapter.

3. As 2 Tim. 2:19 says, "The Lord knows those that are His," and no true believer will ever totally reject the faith (John 10:27–29; Phil. 1:6). But from our human perspective, since we do not know for sure who has been chosen of God and who has not been, we must consider defection a possibility for any person and continue to pray earnestly for everyone (cf. Heb. 3:12–14).

4. Joachim Jeremias, *The Prayers of Jesus* (Philadelphia: Fortress, 1978), 66.

5. Ibid., 72.

6. Ibid., 75.

7. Charles Spurgeon, "Pray Without Ceasing" from *The C. H. Spurgeon Collection*, CD-ROM produced by Ages Software, Inc., 1998.

8. Rom. 1:8; 1 Cor. 1:4; Eph. 1:16; Phil. 1:3; Col. 1:3; 1 Thess. 1:2; 2 Thess. 1:3; 2 Tim. 1:3; Philem. 4.

INDEX OF SCRIPTURE

271

272

Wayne A. Mack (M.Div., Philadelphia Theological Seminary; D.Min., Westminster Theological Seminary) serves as professor of biblical counseling at Grace School of Ministry in Pretoria, South Africa, where he also conducts conferences and seminars. For part of the year, he teaches at The Expositor's Seminary and the Ministry Training School of the Bible Church of Little Rock, Arkansas.

Dr. Mack is adjunct professor of biblical counseling at The Master's College and director of Strengthening Ministries International. He is an executive board member of F.I.R.E. (Fellowship of Independent Reformed Evangelicals) and a charter member and executive board member of the National Association of Nouthetic Counselors. Mack is also a member of the board of directors of the missionary agency Publicaciones Faro de Gracia.

He is the author of numerous books, including *A Fight to the Death*; *Humility*; *Reaching the Ear of God*; *Strengthening Your Marriage*; *Down, but Not Out*; and *Your Family, God's Way*.

David Swavely (M.Div., The Master's Seminary) is a teaching elder in the Presbyterian Church in America. He was the founding pastor of Faith Church in Sonoma, California, and he is currently planting a church in the Malvern area near Philadelphia.

He has also written *Decisions, Decisions: How (and How Not) to Make Them*, and *Who Are You to Judge? The Dangers of Judging and Legalism*. He coauthored, with Harry L. Reeder, *From Embers to a Flame: How God Can Revitalize Your Church*.

ALSO BY WAYNE MACK

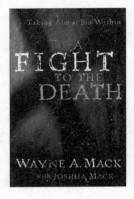

Price: $10.99
To order, visit
www.prpbooks.com
or call
1(800) 631-0094

"With the exegetical precision of John Owen and the practical animation of John Bunyan, Wayne Mack and Joshua Mack make one of the most neglected and misunderstood doctrines today—the mortification of sin—accessible and livable. No pastor, church leader, or member can afford to ignore this title!"

—JERRY MARCELLINO
Pastor and moderator of the Fellowship of Independent Reformed
Evangelicals (FIRE)

"Sin is not a popular subject, but just as a cancer patient needs to learn about his disease, every sinner needs to understand the seriousness of his condition and its cure. The Macks' treatment of sin is thorough, biblical, and practical."

—JAMES NEWHEISER
Pastor, Grace Bible Church, Escondido, CA

"*A Fight to the Death* is well written, practical, and above all, biblical. The Macks do not want you to become spiritual road kill. Buy it, use it, and you will, by God's grace, defeat the unholy trinity of the world, the flesh, and the devil. The right read about an eternally important choice."

—GEORGE C. SCIPIONE
Director of the Institute for Biblical Counseling and Discipleship

ALSO BY WAYNE MACK

Price: $10.99
To order, visit
www.prpbooks.com
or call
1(800) 631-0094

"It's always with confidence and joy that I recommend Wayne Mack's books. He's so thorough and so thoroughly biblical that, when you read them, you know you've just spent valuable time with our Lord and his powerful Word."

—ELYSE FITZPATRICK
Author and counselor

"Sometimes a book reads you while you are reading it. This is that kind of book. It has eyes!"

—JIM ELLIFF
President of Christian Communicators Worldwide

"Wayne and Joshua Mack do an excellent job of diagnosing the cancer of pride and providing inspired biblical treatment. With the scalpel of Scripture they carefully do surgery on the reader's soul. Drawing wisdom from biblical examples and great preachers of the past, they offer practical instruction for extracting pride and replacing it with its counterpart—humility."

—JACK HUGHES
Senior Pastor, Calvary Bible Church,
Adjunct Professor of Homiletics at The Master's Seminary

ALSO BY DAVE SWAVELY

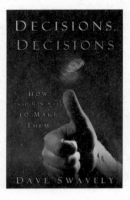

Price: $11.99
To order, visit
www.prpbooks.com
or call
1(800) 631-0094

"Biblical, thoughtful, captivating, and well written. I heartily endorse it as a valuable instrument for your spiritual maturity and discipleship ministry to others.

—HARRY L. REEDER III

"A helpful book that will keep many from going astray. It will fortify those who wish to preserve the integrity of biblical revelation over against others who falsely lay claim to additional revelation. Get it, enjoy it, believe it!"

—JAY ADAMS

"A provocative treatment of a most difficult subject. As a pastor, I have searched for a book on decision making that is biblically precise, yet practically insightful; I now have one."

—LANCE QUINN